Cambridge Elements ≡

Elements in Ame
edited
France
Princeton l

FALSE ALARM

The Truth about Political Mistruths in the Trump Era

Ethan Porter
George Washington University

Thomas J. Wood
Ohio State University

CAMBRIDGE
UNIVERSITY PRESS

CAMBRIDGE
UNIVERSITY PRESS

University Printing House, Cambridge CB2 8BS, United Kingdom

One Liberty Plaza, 20th Floor, New York, NY 10006, USA

477 Williamstown Road, Port Melbourne, VIC 3207, Australia

314–321, 3rd Floor, Plot 3, Splendor Forum, Jasola District Centre,
New Delhi – 110025, India

79 Anson Road, #06–04/06, Singapore 079906

Cambridge University Press is part of the University of Cambridge.

It furthers the University's mission by disseminating knowledge in the pursuit of
education, learning, and research at the highest international levels of excellence.

www.cambridge.org
Information on this title: www.cambridge.org/9781108705929
DOI: 10.1017/9781108688338

First published 2019

A catalogue record for this publication is available from the British Library.

ISBN 978-1-108-70592-9 Paperback
ISBN 978-1-108-68833-8 (online)
ISSN 2515-1606 (online)
ISSN 2515-1592 (print)

False Alarm

The Truth about Political Mistruths in the Trump Era

Elements in American Politics

DOI: 10.1017/9781108688338
First published online: September 2019

Ethan Porter
George Washington University

Thomas J. Wood
Ohio State University

Abstract: Americans are not invulnerable to factual information. They do not "backfire"; facts do not make them less accurate. Instead, they become more accurate, even when corrections target co-partisans. Corrections of fake news yield similar results. Among Republicans, Trump's misstatements are less susceptible to corrections than identical misstatements attributed to other Republicans. While we do not observe facts affecting attitudes, multiple instances of misinformation can increase approval of the responsible politician – but corrections can reduce approval by similar amounts. While corrections do not eliminate false beliefs, they reduce the share of inaccurate beliefs among subjects in this study nearly in half.

Keywords: misinformation, backfire effect, fake news, public opinion

ISBNs: 9781108705929 (PB), ISBN 9781108688338 (OC)
ISSNs: 2515-1606 (online), 2515-1592 (print)

Contents

1 Introduction

The rise of Donald Trump has prompted a panic about the role of facts in American politics. "Facts may be dead," concluded a Brookings Institution report on the rise of "post-truth" America (Glasser 2016). The *Oxford English Dictionary* selected "post-truth" as its word of the year in 2016. "It's time to give up on facts," declared *Slate* after Trump's inauguration (Zimmerman 2017). Other news organizations issued similarly dire proclamations. According to many observers, when it comes to politics, people are nonresponsive to factual information. Instead, at least in America, politics are dominated by partisan hallucinations and fake news, with elected officials and partisan media spreading mistruths that voters eagerly lap up.

Or so the story goes. The evidence we have gathered, however, strongly indicates otherwise. Ordinary people are quite willing to be made more accurate about political facts – even when doing so prompts them to disagree with officials from their preferred political party. In our studies, corrections reduced the share of inaccurate respondents nearly in half. Increased factual accuracy does not have a pronounced partisan or ideological basis; conservative Republicans and liberal Democrats respond to the facts similarly, though not identically. But when the facts correct misstatements uttered by the president they support, even the average Trump voter has responded by becoming more accurate. This has generally been the case during the election and well into the Trump presidency.

All this, however, does not mean that political facts regularly cause people to change their political beliefs – far from it. While Trump voters can be made more accurate by corrections to Trump's misstatements, this increased accuracy does not dampen their enthusiasm for him. Democrats behave no differently. When it comes to political attitudes, facts have limited persuasive capacity. But we are not living in a post-truth world. Facts may not be as pivotal to political attitude formation as some observers might believe them to be. But the panic about facts in American political life is itself not in correspondence with the facts.

This panic is also not entirely new. It is instead an updated version of a set of concerns that has cropped up regularly in American history. Often but not always, these concerns have been voiced in times of tumult. During World War II, philosopher Alexander Koyre asserted, "Never has there been so much lying as in our day" (Koyre 1945, p. 290). Nearly thirty years later, the release of the Pentagon Papers prompted Hannah Arendt to deplore the "extent to which lying was permitted to proliferate throughout the ranks of all governmental services" and to argue that political lies have more persuasive power than political truths (Arendt 1971, p. 4). Summing up American politics in the aftermath of the Watergate scandal, a writer for *The Nation* magazine argued, "In a very fundamental way we, as a free people, have freely decided that we want to live in some post-truth world" (Teisch 1992, p. 13).

From the moment he announced his presidential candidacy, Donald Trump has proven unafraid to utter falsehoods. It seems as if he perceives there to be no consequences for his lying. As he once infamously mused, he could "shoot someone in the middle of Fifth Avenue" and not lose voters. If he thinks his supporters would support him even in those circumstances, it only makes sense that he thinks they would support him when his statements bear no relationship to empirical evidence.

In this Element, we describe a set of experiments administered during the 2016 campaign and two years into the Trump presidency. The experiments were designed to evaluate how ordinary Americans react to political lies and political truths. Most of the experiments proceeded by showing people at least one political mistruth, randomly assigning some of those people to see a factual correction that rebuts the mistruth and then measuring agreement with the proposition advanced by the initial mistruth. By comparing levels of agreement between those who were assigned to see a factual correction and those who were not, we arrived at measures of the capacity of facts to repudiate mistruths.

We have repeatedly found that the average effect of factual corrections on false beliefs is in the direction of more accuracy – that is, on average, people respond to factual corrections by becoming more accurate. This has been the case even when the correction cuts against the preferred political party or ideology of respondents. We have observed this behavior across a broad array of issues, from technical policy matters to those that usually provoke sharp disagreement along partisan lines. We have also tested and detected similar effects when people see corrections to "fake news," or false news stories, including among partisans whom the story flatters. Our experiments have been carried out over nonrepresentative internet panels and internet panels designed to achieve higher levels of representativeness, as well as over the phone. While corrections do not increase accuracy about every single subject, across all our experiments, we find that they reduce the share of people who believe inaccurate information by 28 percentage points.

We have uncovered little evidence that corrections can change political beliefs. In our experiments, citizens who are made more accurate by corrections to misstatements made by their party's leaders subsequently exhibited no change in support for their party's leaders and policies. This is not to say that corrective information *never* changes political attitudes. Indeed, we find that a sufficient volume of correction information can marginally depress approval of the candidate advancing the misinformation. When *not* accompanied by a correction, the same high volume of misinformation can move approval in a slightly positive direction. Politicians have incentive to spread mistruths only if they are certain that they can keep ahead of the fact-checkers. We have failed to uncover strong evidence that correction effects last. Across a variety of fake news items, we find that accuracy gains mostly dissipate shortly after exposure to a correction.

In a highly polarized, hyper-partisan age, the failure of individual corrections and individual misstatements to move political attitudes should not be as surprising as it might sound. A long literature attests to the overwhelming power of partisanship in American political attitudes (e.g., Green, Palmquist, and Schickler 2002). Partisans express deep animus toward counter-partisans, with consequences for support for interparty marriage (Iyengar, Sood, and Lelkes 2012) and a range of broader social identities (Mason 2018). Given their depth of devotion, people do not set aside their party's political candidates or policies lightly. But we are not living in a post-truth age. Contingent upon seeing the facts, people of all political stripes can, in most cases, become measurably more accurate.

To be clear, without a correction, many people express inaccurate beliefs. Without a correction, conservatives were generally less accurate than liberals. But after a correction, across our experiments, only 24.7 percent of our subjects offered inaccurate responses. Correction sliced the share of inaccurate responses nearly in half, with large reductions in inaccuracy across political perspectives. And while subjects were often more eager to correct counter-partisans than co-partisans, we still observed large gains in accuracy among subjects whose co-partisans were corrected.

A High-stakes Question

The question motivating our work – how do most people respond to political facts, even when the facts are unwelcome? – has been asked by many social scientists before us. With good reason: answers to this question help shed light on the very feasibility of democracy. Democratic citizens, it has been argued, must have a wellspring of political knowledge upon which to draw as they (a) suss out their own interests and (b) try to hold elected officials accountable for advancing those interests (e.g., Carpini and Keeter 1996; Kuklinski et al. 2000; Hochschild and Einstein 2015). In the memorable phrasing of Carpini and Keeter (1996, p. 8), "political information ... is the currency of democratic citizenship." Without political information, or with wildly inaccurate information – misinformation – citizens may not be able to identify whether or not their interests are being served, and which policy makers they should alternately reward or punish.

Consider, for the sake of illustration, a citizen who loses her job because of a policy decision. If the citizen knows that a policy decision was responsible, and if she can accurately identify a responsible policy maker, she may be able to hold that policy maker accountable. On the other hand, if the citizen is ignorant of both the policy decision and its progenitor, accountability will be difficult to come by. Going further, imagine that the citizen is told that the party with which she identifies is responsible for her job loss. Not conceding this factual point would not bode well for her, or democracy more broadly.

Accurate political information is a prerequisite for more basic political tasks as well. The act of voting requires that one be aware of the date of the election and the location at which one may cast a ballot. Upon entering the voting booth, one is required to express preferences about a range of candidates and, oftentimes, ballot issues. Supporting a policy and imploring your neighbor to do so as well usually require some reservoir of political facts. Deciding to attend a protest or other political event depends on having accurate knowledge of where and when the event will take place.

A great deal of research has concluded that if political information is the currency of democratic citizenship, then the United States is near bankruptcy. Americans are misinformed about many basic political facts, such as the meaning of ideological terms, the identities of elected officials, and details of the policy debates of the day (e.g., Berelson et al. 1954; Campbell et al. 1960; Achen and Bartels 2016). Though the numbers wax and wane, the American National Election Study (ANES) has consistently reported that many Americans cannot accurately say who controls Congress; a majority was wrong on this question as recently as 2008 (ANES 2018).

Some of the difficulty in acquiring accurate political knowledge can probably be attributed to partisanship. In *The American Voter*, Campbell and co-authors (1960) describe citizens as bringing a "perceptual screen" to politics, through which partisanship and ideology operate. This screen can prevent people from learning political facts that endanger or otherwise cut against their political commitments. Some work has found new examples of this phenomenon (e.g., Jerit and Barabas 2012). Partisans make strikingly different evaluations of the national economy, including when they are asked to estimate objective measures (e.g., Bartels 2002). Partisanship communicates to people which policies they should support and which they should oppose (e.g., Lenz 2012). Partisans interpret the unemployment rate in a partisan-consistent manner (Schaffner and Roche 2017); partisanship also colors interpretations of the Iraq War casualty figures (Gaines, Kuklinski, Quirk, Peyton, and Verkuilen 2007).

Partisan polarization – the distance in attitudes and perceptions between adherents of the two parties – has only increased with time (e.g., Abramowitz 2010). "Floating voters," whose partisan allegiances shift with each election and who once made up a sizable proportion of the American electorate (Zaller 2004), have sharply declined in number (Smidt 2017). Partisans now harbor remarkable levels of animus against rank-and-file members of the other party. According to some scholars, discrimination against members of the opposite party can be more powerful than race-based discrimination (e.g., Iyengar and Westwood 2015). Americans are now so wedded to their partisan identities (Mason 2018) that discrimination against members of the other party can emerge in distinctly apolitical contexts, such as the buying and selling of football tickets (Engelhardt and Utych 2018).

Increases in partisan polarization have hardly stanched the flow of political information. Ardent partisans and committed moderates alike are confronted ceaselessly with political information. For partisans, some of this information may be unwelcome. It may undermine claims made by one of their party's leaders. It may show that when in power, their party was not particularly successful at governing. If they are shown information that corrects false claims made by their leaders, they may have to concede that their leaders are dissemblers or even liars.

As partisan polarization has increased, so too have media attempts to correct political misinformation. Commonly known as "fact-checking," this practice is now undertaken by numerous prominent outlets, such as the *Washington Post*, the Associated Press, and the *New York Times*. Many websites, such as PolitiFact.com and Snopes.com, exist largely for the same purpose. The rise of fact-checking is a relatively new phenomenon (Graves 2016). Yet while it may be edifying for some of those who consume it, there is good reason to think its effects will be limited at best. "People … resist correct information," conclude Kuklinski et al. (2000, p. 809).

Yet resistance is not even the worst-case scenario. Upon encountering corrective information, it is possible that people go so far as to *reject* the new information altogether and strengthen their commitment to the initial misinformation. This so-called backfire effect, as described in Nyhan and Reifler (2010), may be especially powerful when the corrective facts conflict with their broader political beliefs, such as those relating to party affiliation and ideology. The backfire effect, which we describe at length in the Section 2, proposes that factually accurate information will provoke some people to become *less* accurate.

Psychology offers some evidence that would seem to lay the groundwork for the backfire effect. In the 1970s, Loftus and colleagues argued that exposure to faulty information about an event witnessed by participants can debilitate accurate descriptions of those events. For example, subjects who saw a video of a car racing along a road without a barn and were then asked a question that alluded to a barn were more likely to believe a week later that indeed a barn had been visible in the video they had seen (Loftus and Palmer 1974; Loftus 1975). Some of this same research, however, found that misinformation could be rejected. For example, subjects presented with "blatantly" misinformed descriptions of what they had just seen were overwhelmingly likely to reject such a description (Loftus 1979). In those studies, subjects rejected misinformation on their own accord, without being exposed to a correction.

When factual corrections are administered, misinformation does not necessarily disappear. The "continued influence effect" describes the extent to which corrected misinformation can still influence subsequent beliefs (e.g., Johnson and Siefert 1998). This effect has mostly been measured in terms of subjects' reliance on the corrected misinformation when responding to subsequent questions (e.g., Ecker et al. 2010). The continued influence effect, however, can be mitigated; Ecker et al. (2010) find that subjects who receive a general warning about the ability of false information to affect beliefs become less reliant on false information. Yet the authors note that even though the warnings work, misinformation still "lingered to a significant degree" (Ecker et al. 2010, p. 1096). As Loftus puts it, "The argument has been advanced more than once that new information can cause a restructuring of cognitive representation that is quite irreversible" (Loftus 1979, p. 373).

We are not so pessimistic. When it comes to political information, we believe that despite the enormous increase in partisan polarization, the average citizen can respond to corrections of misinformation by becoming more factually accurate. *All* citizens will *not* be made more accurate by corrections. But the average citizen will.

Accuracy and Partisanship, Simultaneously

In their path-breaking work on motivated political reasoning, Charles Taber and Milton Lodge describe two possible ways citizens can respond to unwelcome political facts. Citizens can pursue *accuracy* goals, whereby they are compelled to "seek out and carefully consider relevant evidence so as to reach a correct or otherwise best conclusion." Alternately, they can pursue *partisan* goals, whereby they "apply their reasoning powers in defense of a prior, specific conclusion" (Lodge and Taber 2006, p. 756; 2013, p. 150). If they chase accuracy, citizens will respond by learning without bias; if they pursue directional goals, they will respond in a manner consistent with the political biases they had previously.

We propose that citizens can pursue both at once. When they encounter factual information that impugns or otherwise challenges claims made by their party, the typical citizen will be wiling to pursue an accuracy goal, even as doing so causes them to implicitly distance themselves from a co-partisan's claim. Yet the pursuit of accuracy is limited *only* to the factual matter at stake. Questions related to vote choice and policy attitudes, which expressly ask them to reflect their partisanship, are more likely to activate the pursuit of partisan goals. The average American can and does pursue both goals – chasing after accuracy regarding discrete factual matters while also pursuing partisan goals when asked, directly, about their partisanship. Essentially, this is a dual-processing model, in line with copious research testifying to individuals' ability to vary the level of cognitive effort they put toward particular tasks (see Evans 2008 for a review). Level of effort varies with the motivation and the cost of information acquisition; high motivation and low costs will compel more effort, and vice versa (Rahn 1993, p. 475).

The imperative of reflecting factual reality has been recognized since Festinger. As he puts it, "Elements of cognition are responsive to reality. ... It would be unlikely that an organism could live and survive if the elements of cognition were not to a large extent a verdical map of reality" (Festinger 1957, p. 10). When they encounter challenging factually corrective information, people could go to great lengths to resist it. They could strenuously counter-argue, conceiving of ample reasons to reject the correction before them. This, in turn, could cause them to brush off the correction or, as backfire posits, become more committed to the initial false claim.

Crucially, however, the extent to which people are interested in reconciling contradictory kinds of information depends on how much they value the different items at play (Festinger 1957, p. 17). In the political context, reconciling the misleading claim of a co-partisan with the correction that follows may not be especially important. Consequently, when confronted with corrections, they may respond by *easily* becoming more accurate, to keep their mental map in correspondence with the world around them. Yet their partisan preferences remain untouched. What they value less changes more easily. Partisan-motivated reasoning requires the exertion of effort (Lodge and Taber 2006, p. 757) – effort that people would prefer *not* to spend about questions relating to basic factual accuracy. Compared to their partisanship, they are less invested in facts; this discrepancy permits them to pursue both accuracy and directional goals at once.

As prior scholars have emphasized, the desire to hold correct views is widespread and fundamental (e.g., Festinger 1950, 1957; Petty and Cacciopo 1986). Indeed, people's willingness to be made more accurate by corrections while remaining committed to their party allows them to hold "correct" views in two ways. First, by responding to unwelcome corrective information by being made more accurate, people's views are correct in the sense that they more closely reflect the world around them. Second, by not subsequently changing their views about co-partisan politicians and policies, people are also correct, here in the sense that their views remain consistent with their partisanship. If partisan allegiance functions like allegiance to a sports team or a religion, as some have put it (e.g., Green, Palmquist, and Schickler 2002), then it only makes sense that this allegiance will not be shaken by one corrective fact.

Whether this bodes well for democracy depends on one's normative views. To return to the illustrative example offered earlier, by the implication of our argument, a citizen who loses her job due to actions taken by her own party could conceivably acknowledge her party's responsibility. Yet we do not have reason to believe that her support for her party would diminish.[1] On the one hand, that she is made more accurate by corrections would indicate that the public *can* become more informed about politics. On the other hand, her failure to draw upon this new information when forming political attitudes suggests that citizens do not live up to the ideal of democratic citizenship, wherein empirical evidence precedes political accountability.

The Ease of Factual Corrections

One key component of our argument is that people can *easily* be made more factually accurate about political matters. However, prior claims about the innate appeal of empirical accuracy (e.g., Festinger 1950, 1957; Petty and Cacciopo 1986) have not focused on political matters. It may be the case that the appeal of accuracy is reduced when politics enter the picture. When our partisan loyalties are activated, perhaps holding accurate views is less important. Do politics encourage greater resistance to correction than other topics?

An experiment we conducted in March 2019 offers insight. We exposed participants over Amazon's Mechanical Turk to a variety of common false claims about politics and nonpolitical topics. For politics, we looked for recent misstatements made by politicians from both sides of the aisle. For example, we featured a claim by prominent Democratic congresswoman Alexandra Ocasio-

---

[1] For experimental evidence on possible responses, consult Huber, Hill, and Lenz (2012).

Cortez, in which she said: "Unemployment is low because everyone has two jobs. Unemployment is low because people are working 60, 70, 80 hours a week and can barely feed their family" (Jacobson 2018). We then randomly assigned some subjects to see a factual correction, which pointed out unemployment data includes everyone who works more than ten hours a week across jobs. All subjects were then asked to agree or disagree with the following: "Unemployment is low because people are forced to work multiple jobs." On a 1–5 scale, possible answers ranged from "Strongly disagree" to "Strongly agree." We also tested recent misstatements by President Trump, Congresswoman Lynne Cheney, and White House Press Secretary Sarah Sanders, testing twelve political misstatements in total. All misstatements and corrections can be found in the online Appendix.

Coming up with common, nonpolitical misperceptions was no easy task. We had to identify widely held false beliefs that lack obvious political stakes and could be targeted with a correction. Most of the nonpolitical misperceptions we tested relate to life's mundane realities. For example, we told some subjects: "Microwaves are a common appliance in most Americans' kitchens. You might have heard the concern that, when food is microwaved in a plastic container, dangerous chemicals can be released into the food." Then, some randomly saw this correction: "This is untrue. In 40 years of research, no one has demonstrated that microwaving food in plastic imparts chemicals." All subjects had to agree, along a 5-point scale, with the following statement: "Microwaving food in a plastic container can release dangerous chemicals into the food."[2] We presented eleven other common, nonpolitical misperceptions, including the notion that gum takes five years to digest, that Napoleon Bonaparte was unusually short, and that toilets flush in different directions in different hemispheres. Subjects were randomly assigned to see eight misstatements each, drawing over both political and nonpolitical issues.

In Figure 1.1, we show correction effects – that is, the effect of being randomly assigned to see a correction – across all political and nonpolitical issues.[3] Figure 1.1 makes several important points. First, our nonpolitical corrections mostly feature no relation to ideology. Second, and more importantly, it shows political misstatements *are about as amenable to correction as apolitical statements.*

---

[2] In this experiment, to maintain consistency between political and nonpolitical issues, we did not invoke sources when issuing corrections.

[3] These models use the same functional form used in Nyhan and Reifler (2010), where an experimental condition indicator is interacted with a continuous control for ideology.

Ideology vs Agreement with Incorrect Claim (5pt scale)

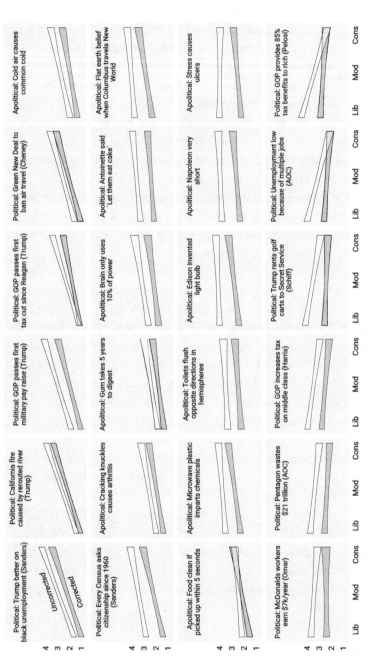

Figure 1.1 Factual adherence for 12 political and 12 apolitical elections. Ribbons indicates the 95 percent confidence intervals for the fitted values by experimental condition and ideology. In each facet, a smaller value indicates an *improvement* in factual accuracy. For political corrections, the associated speaker is depicted inside parentheses. A dark ribbon below a light ribbon indicates a significant improvement in factual accuracy after being corrected. Issues are sorted by the uncorrected subjects' relationship with ideology. Topics are sorted by the ideological slope among uncorrected subjects. "Cheney" refers to Senator Elizabeth Cheney, "Clinton" refers to Hillary Clinton, and

To more rigorously test if both political misinformation and nonpolitical misinformation are comparably correctable, we estimate a mixed model.[4] In Figure 1.2, we show average correction effects including both main and issue-specific factors, averaging over ideology.

Figure 1.2 shows that the *least* correctable misstatement concerned the so-called 5-second rule, which attempts to provide a rule of thumb for how long food can safely touch an unhygienic surface. Across the twenty-four issues of both types, neither was systematically more responsive to interventions. Some psychological research has indicated that counter-ideological information can be sufficiently discomforting so as to prompt subjects to engage in cognitively demanding counter-argument – to counteract the information's unwelcome implications. Our findings cast doubt upon this conclusion. Misstatements that implicate *no political symbols at all* show basically the same responsiveness to corrections. With these results in mind, it would be hasty to assume a separate ideological basis for voters' engagement with political corrections. Rather than implicate a separate, maladaptive response saved for politically threatening information, subjects seem to use the same psychological process for factual responsiveness for mundane and political corrections alike.

These findings corroborate the premise of our argument. So too does the rest of this Element. On no occasion have we observed average subjects responding to corrections by increasing their belief in misinformation. This has been the case even when the corrections cast aspersions on subjects' co-partisans and co-ideologues. Indeed, across all our studies, corrections increase the share of subjects who hold accurate views by 28 percentage points. These findings echo recent work that finds that partisan differences in responses to supposedly objective questions can be exaggerated. Bullock et al. (2015), for example, find that the gap between partisans on knowledge questions diminishes significantly when respondents are paid for accurate responses or to concede that they do not know. Similarly, Prior et al. (2015) show that partisan differences in economic evaluations can also be mitigated when respondents are reminded to provide accurate answers. More closely in conversation with our results, Guess and Coppock (n.d.) present results from experiments designed to elicit backfire (or "backlash," as they call it) among subjects by providing them with

---

[4] The model takes the form of

$$Answer = b_0 + b_1\left(correction_j \times issuetype_k\right) + (b_2 + \eta_1)\left(correction_j \times ideology_i\right) + e_{i,j,k}$$

(1.1)

where j indexes if a respondent saw a correction for a specific issue, k indexes political or nonpolitical issue types, η is a random term allowing for issue specific variation in ideological and correction effects.

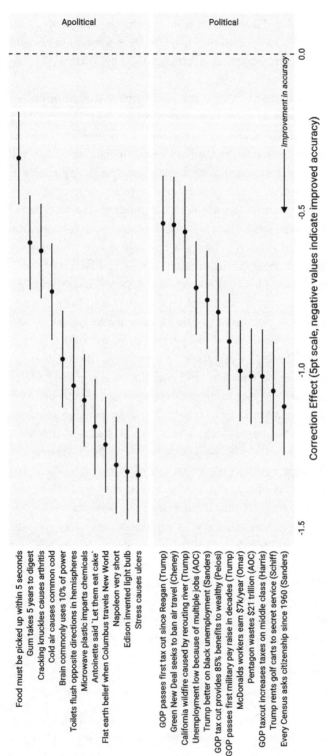

Figure 1.2 Correction effects by issue. These quantities are drawn from Table 1.1 and include both random and fixed effects. Since all misstatements are at least somewhat correctable, all point ranges are significantly negative.

counter-attitudinal information; they conclude that, at most, such a response is exceedingly rare.

The receptivity of citizens to corrections bodes well for the increasingly common journalist practice of fact-checking (Graves 2016). When it comes to the mass public, there is evidence that fact-checks deployed during political debates can increase factual knowledge (Wintersieck 2017). A recent meta-analysis also makes clear that while disseminating misinformation can have powerful effects, so too can the presentation of information meant to correct or "debunk" that misinformation (Chan et al. 2017). In the main, our evidence reinforces this point: fact-checks substantially increase the public's factual accuracy.

Plan of the Element

Section 2 describes and contextualizes many tests we have conducted of what may be the most pessimistic account of how citizens respond to political information: the backfire effect, which posits that facts can actually compound inaccuracies. Since its publication, the canonical research advancing this idea (Nyhan and Reifler 2010) has been cited more than almost any other work in political behavior. Across more than fifty issues and more than 10,000 subjects, we have been unable to detect backfire. During both the 2016 primary and the general election, we observed the average effect of corrections on false beliefs to be negative. This was true even when we provided partisans with corrections that cut against their own candidate.

In Section 3, we focus on fake news, or outlandish, fictitious political stories that have been widely circulated. We show that such stories can also be corrected. For fake news, the average correction effect we observe is in the direction of increased accuracy. A second study answers the following: After people see a correction to fake news, how long are their beliefs more accurate? Our evidence here is more mixed. When we average across all our items, we find little evidence that correction effects last long. When it comes to factual accuracy about fake news, corrections work, but one correction is unlikely to last.

Section 4 focuses on Donald Trump. First, we describe results from experiments conducted when Trump was a candidate. In these experiments, the average subject who saw a correction responded by expressing more accurate views. This was true among Republicans, and it was true when we randomized whether subjects were exposed to Trump campaign officials denigrating the correction provided. We also present experiments about misstatements uttered by Trump as president. Across political affiliations, we again find corrections increasing accuracy, well into his administration. We also investigated whether

Trump is less susceptible to corrections than other Republican politicians. Among conservatives, this seems to be the case. Finally, we look at whether the number of corrections or misstatements affects Trump's approval. We find some evidence that many corrections degrade and many misstatements enhance public approval of his presidency. In no study did we observe average Republicans being made more inaccurate by corrections.

In Section 5, we put our findings in broader perspective. Our portrayal of average Americans' factual receptivity is unusually optimistic. How did observers come to have such a negative impression of voters? We offer several explanations. The inclination to condemn voters as unfit and gullible is a recurrent trend, especially in response to unwelcome political developments. Furthermore, the "crazy uncles" of everyday life – the people who contend that, say, the Illuminati are fostering climate change – are vividly memorable and lead people to overestimate the frequency of fact resistance. But by definition, the crazy uncle is an anomaly: the rest of one's family probably has views at least somewhat tethered to reality. Trump may have turned American politics upside down, but he has not done the same to human psychology. When forming political attitudes, Americans' relationship to facts may not be what researchers or political commentators desire. Yet that relationship is not defined by outright rejection of factual corrections.

2 Facts, the Backfire Effect, and the 2016 Election

When it comes to political misinformation and attempts to correct it, the most pessimistic of all accounts is what is known as "the backfire effect." In everyday speech, when something doesn't go the way we intended it to, it's common to say that that something "backfired." If I try a new recipe and my family doesn't prefer it to the old one, I might say that the new recipe backfired. If a friend suggests a movie to see and I counter with another, the friend might describe his suggestion as having backfired.

In political misinformation research, the backfire effect refers to something more specific: the purported tendency of people to respond to attempts to increase their level of factually accurate beliefs by increasing their commitment to a factually erroneous position. Suppose, for example, that you believe that a president of your preferred political party oversaw a drop in the unemployment rate, while the unemployment rate, in point of fact, actually rose. If I point this discrepancy out to you, you would backfire if you became *more* convinced in your initially false belief. Importantly, the effect is not about attempts to make people more accurate that don't succeed. Backfire occurs when such attempts achieve the *inverse* of their intention.

In political science, Brendan Nyhan and Jason Reifler (2010) conducted the canonical study of backfire. American history is replete with panics about citizens' ability to discern information from misinformation. The Iraq War prompted one such panic. The Bush administration argued that one of the reasons for war was related to Iraq's supposed production of weapons of mass destruction (WMDs) – weapons that were never found. Nyhan and Reifler leveraged the administration's claims about WMDs, and a subsequent government report contradicting the claim, to test receptivity to facts.

Within a longer newspaper article, participants in Nyhan and Reifler's study saw the following claim by President Bush: "There was a risk, a real risk, that Saddam Hussein would pass weapons or materials or information to terrorist networks, and in the world after September the 11th, that was a risk we could not afford to take" (Nyhan and Reifler 2010). Some participants were also told in the newspaper article about the Duelfer Report, which concluded that Iraq had lacked a WMD program. All participants were then asked to agree with the proposition that prior to the war, Iraq had a WMD program.

For some participants, the Duelfer Report did its job: after reading about it, they became more likely to agree that Iraq had had no WMD program. But that wasn't the case for everyone. Conservatives who were told about the report became more likely to say that Iraq had a program. The accurate information didn't just bounce off them; it made them more inaccurate. For conservatives, the report backfired. Backfire wasn't limited to WMDs; Nyhan and Reifler also observed a backfire effect on the relationship between tax cuts and tax receipts.

What made conservatives exhibit backfire? There are at least two explanations. First, as conservatives, they were likely protective of conservative policies and politicians, viewing them as essential to their political and partisan identities. For the average conservative, being made more accurate would amount to breaking with their partisan identities. As a long literature shows, people are hesitant to do just that, as they attach great importance to their parties of choice (e.g., Green, Palmquist, and Schickler 2002; Achen and Bartels 2016). The second explanation relates to their stations in life: Nyhan and Reifler's participants were all college students. College students are unusual in their willingness to exert cognitive resources (Petty, Cacioppo, and Morris 1983). When confronted with unwelcome political facts, college students might think extensively about how to respond. Seeing their political beliefs challenged, they might respond by rejecting the factual information in favor of their political beliefs.

It's difficult to overstate the influence of Nyhan and Reifler's article. Over the past ten years, it has been the most highly cited article from the journal *Political*

Behavior.[5] Its conclusions have seeped into other disciplines. A team of neuroscientists concluded that the brains of people who were exposed to policy arguments that challenged their political beliefs, and who resisted this new information, looked different than the brains of people who did not (Kaplan, Gimbel, and Harris 2016). As late as 2019, computer scientists were offering mathematical models of public opinion spread that included the backfire effect (Chin et al. 2019). Media commentators, including the host of *Meet the Press*, have talked about the finding. An NPR program intended to popularize social science featured a symposium of backfire papers in September 2017. In the same year, a TV program normally dedicated to debunking myths, *Adam Ruins Everything*, spent an episode describing backfire. In 2018, an art exhibit at the Tate Modern was inspired by it (Cordrea-Rado 2018). Wolfgang Tillmans, the artist responsible for the exhibit, understood the stakes. If large numbers of people "are resistant to rational argument, we are on a slippery slope," he wrote in *The Guardian* (Tillmans 2018).

Indeed, backfire stands out for its depressing implications about citizen competence for democracy. When applied to our running illustration of the citizen who has been laid off, backfire proposes that if the citizen has been told of the responsible policy maker, the citizen would respond by believing the opposite. Holding that policy maker accountable would thus be impossible. In Figure 2.1, we offer an approximate depiction of some popular descriptions of citizens' cognitive processes and their implications for democratic purposes. Of course, this figure does not exhaustively include all existing descriptions. But it does incorporate several of the more influential accounts. The figure is also not meant to be mathematically exact. It is meant to distill the theoretical stakes of this research.

At the top right of Figure 2.1, we place the three theories that expect citizens to be objective processors of information, all of which bode well for democracy. Spatial voting, which can be traced back to Downs (1957), regards individual citizens as making political calculations based on their spatial congruence to the choices before them. Similarly, Bayesian models (e.g., Hill 2017) depict individuals as successfully updating in response to new information. Some mid-level descriptions, which can broadly be described as the "Michigan school," regard citizens as somewhat but not entirely responsive to factual information. Citizens may not be immaculate vessels of accurate information, but they can make politically meaningful decisions with the information that they have (e.g., Lupia 1994). This also accords with the "perceptual screen" perspective,

---

[5] As of April 2019, the backfire paper has been cited 1,132 times. The second-most cited contemporary paper from this journal has 235.

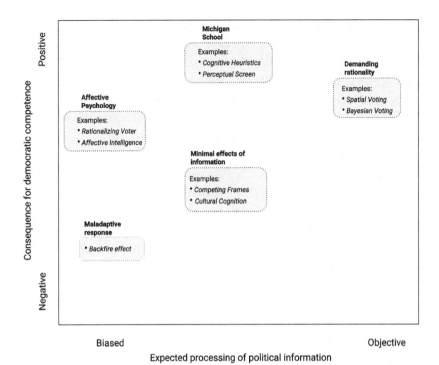

Figure 2.1 An approximation.

described earlier, which does not foreclose responsiveness to information (Campbell et al. 1960).

Other theories, particularly those closer to the nexus of psychology and political behavior, construe citizens as motivated reasoners (e.g., Lodge and Taber 2013), who sometimes arrive at factually accurate conclusions while applying partisan-consistent interpretations (e.g., Gaines and Kuklinski 2007). Similarly, "affective intelligence" describes citizens as heavily swayed by their emotions, though not entirely at the expense of unbiased information (e.g., Marcus, Neuman, and Marcus 2000).

Those accounts that are more pessimistic for democracy leave even less room for non-biased information processing. One argument holds that elite framing explains most political beliefs (e.g., Chong and Druckman 2007). Cultural cognition, as advanced by Kahan and colleagues (e.g., Kahan and Braman 2006), proposes that factual beliefs are inescapably tied up with sociocultural identities. In their understanding, citizens are only "receptive to sound empirical evidence [if] policy bears a social meaning congenial to their cultural values" (Kahan and Braman 2006, p. 169).

Yet only the backfire effect proposes *more* than nonresponsiveness – it proposes responsiveness in the opposite direction. None of the other schools of thought portrayed here preclude some level of responsiveness. Even cultural cognition allows for circumstances under which accurate facts matter. The backfire effect is at the bottom left in the figure, and for good reason. Backfire proposes something far stronger than the notion that the perceptual screen of partisanship colors interpretations or that receptiveness to accuracy covaries with cultural values. Under backfire, facts themselves compound factual inaccuracies, not just the interpretation of those facts.

If backfire exists, it is likely related to the impulse to counter-argument. It is possible that a highly accordant correction-misstatement pair, where a correction provides an unambiguous, direct contradiction to a misstatement, is especially threatening to ideologues, encouraging respondents to be most resistant.

If real and widespread, the backfire effect bodes poorly for democracy and citizen competence. But is it real? Several studies other than Nyhan and Reifler (2010) have identified instances of what appears as backfire (e.g., Berinsky 2015). Nyhan and Reifler found that giving people corrective information about so- called death panels created by the Affordable Care Act worked at dissuading people from believing such falsehoods – except if participants were politically knowledgeable supporters of former Alaska governor Sarah Palin, who had endorsed the myth. Those participants backfired, coming to believe more strongly that deaths panels did exist (Nyhan, Reifler, and Ubel 2013).[6]

Searching for Backfire during the 2016 Election

As the 2016 election unfolded, we attempted to measure the prevalence of backfire. Our initial impulse was straightforward. The influential studies of backfire had identified the effect exclusively among conservatives. According to the available evidence, liberals did not become less accurate when presented with corrections of co-partisans. We intended to test the limits of this finding.

Try as we might, we never provoked any ideological group to backfire. Regardless of whether or not the information conflicted or corresponded to their political beliefs, in all our studies, corrections increased the average participant's accuracy. To be sure, as we'll see in Sections 3 and 4, Democrats were not as affected in the direction of accuracy by information that cut against Democrats, and Republicans were not as affected by information that cut against Republicans. But on no issue did the average liberal, conservative, or moderate become *misinformed* after reading a correction that contradicted a political affiliate.

---

[6] Other studies, such as Berinsky (2015), have looked at the relationship between factual information and attitudes and have also found what they sometimes describe as a backfire or backlash effect. We might think of such backfire as attitudinal backfire, distinct from factual backfire.

We conducted five experiments, enrolling more than 10,000 people and testing more than fifty examples of potential backfire. Like Nyhan and Reifler, sometimes we embedded factual corrections in mocked-up news articles; sometimes, we simply presented participants with statements and corrections. All the examples of misstatements came from real incidents involving political leaders from both parties making claims at odds with empirical evidence.[7]

For our first experiment, we identified eight misstatements made by politicians, four from each party. We wanted to test issues that we thought would be most prone to induce backfire. We wanted issues that were highly politically charged. Among the universe of social facts, a small few have any meaningful political consequence; most have not been the subject of sustained elite disagreement. For such issues, telling an ideologue that their preferred politician misspoke should not induce a willingness to psychologically resist or counter-argue, because the fact has no unwelcome consequence for the recipient. Instead, we chose issues that had been the recurrent subject of political debate.

To ensure that these corrections were on issues prone to induce backfire, we chose topics in light of those Americans identify when asked: "What do you think is the most important problem facing this country today?" Figure 2.2 shows the distribution of answers on this question among 131,100 respondents asked this question on 118 separate surveys administered between 1996 and 2015, as measured by the Roper Center. Figure 2.2 shows our corrections are disproportionately on those topics deemed highly important. We also achieve broad coverage of issues. Among the 30 issues most reliably cited as being important, we corrected misconceptions on 21.

To further pique subjects' ideological loyalties, we corrected speakers who were national figures, either as aspirants for the presidency or prominent legislators.[8] A figure whose ideological loyalties are unclear to a subject is unlikely to inspire counter-argument when contradicted. Instead, we corrected figures who are at the apex of their respective ideological cohorts. For instance,

---

[7] Formally, each experiment was an adapted Latin squares design (Cochran and Cox, 1960):

$$
\begin{array}{cccc}
T_1 & T_2 & \cdots & T_J \\
T_2 & T_3 & & \vdots \\
\vdots & & \ddots & \\
T_J & \cdots & & T_1
\end{array}
$$

in which j indexes the total number of treatments in some study, the rows indicate the order in which a respondent saw each treatment, and the columns indicate the possible permutations of treatments.

[8] The one exception to this was the correction to the National Rifle Association's executive director, Wayne LaPierre.

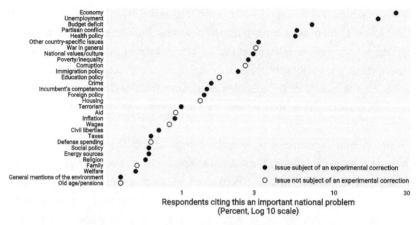

Figure 2.2 Perceptions of the most important national problems, 2006–2015. Solid points indicate that the problem was included in our experiments.

Source: Roper Center's Most Important Problem data set.

among liberals, we corrected then-incumbent President Barack Obama, and both of the leading Democratic candidates to replace him (Secretary Hillary Clinton and Senator Bernie Sanders). Among conservatives, we corrected the leading Republican presidential aspirants (Donald Trump, Ted Cruz, Ben Carson, and Marco Rubio) and Speaker Paul Ryan.

For example, we featured a claim by Clinton that the "epidemic of gun violence knows no boundaries, knows no limits, of any kind," implying that the incidence of gun homicides had been increasing. In fact, available data shows exactly the opposite: gun homicides have declined precipitously in recent decades, after adjusting for the change in the population over that period. Likewise, we corrected Rubio, a Republican presidential aspirant and US senator, claiming "Defense spending has fallen dramatically on President Obama's watch." This was contradicted by the Department of Defense, which showed defense spending rising in the Obama administration compared to the previous administration. As we wanted to see if corrections could increase accuracy even in the presence of partisanship, we identified each speaker's partisanship.

For each misstatement, subjects were then randomly assigned to see – or not see – a correction. All corrections pointed to available government data. For example, for the Rubio claim, subjects assigned to a correction saw the following: "In fact, according to the Defense Department, defense spending under President Obama is higher than it was under President George W. Bush." For the Clinton claim, subjects assigned to the correction saw: "In fact, according to the FBI, the number of gun homicides has fallen since the mid 1990s, declining by about 50% between 1994 and 2013." All corrections in this study took a similar form, succinctly rebutting the claim made by the politician by pointing to evidence from a neutral source.

We then asked all subjects to agree with the position advanced by the initial misstatement, on a five-point scale. To understand how it worked, consider an example from Study 1. First, subjects saw this false claim: "Defense spending has fallen dramatically on President Obama's watch, and our forces have been reduced and suffered readiness challenges even as threats abroad increase. Our military therefore needs a serious program of reinvestment and modernization." The claim was attributed to "Senator Marco Rubio (R-FL) 'Campaign Rally: My Plan to Restore American Strength', Manchester NH, November 5 2015." Those assigned a correction then saw: "In fact, according to the Defense Department, defense spending under President Obama is higher than it was under President George W. Bush." Finally, all subjects were asked: "Do you agree or disagree with the following statement?" and shown the following: "Defense spending under President Barack Obama is lower than it was under President Bush." Possible answers ranged from "Strongly disagree" to "Strongly agree" on a five-point scale. The complete text of all misstatements, corrections and survey items appears in the online Appendix.[9]

Figure 2.3 shows that we were unable to induce backfire for any of the eighteen combinations of ideological cohort and corrections. Across the ideological spectrum, the average ideologue was made more accurate by corrections, even when they contradicted an ally. To get a better sense of these corrections' magnitude, compare the horizontal difference between corrected and uncorrected subjects to the total ideological effect among uncorrected respondents. This is a coarse measure of these corrections' influence, compared to the underlying ideological differences on these highly charged issues. The mean difference between uncorrected liberals and conservatives, averaging across issues, was 1.1 on a five-point scale. The mean correction effect, meanwhile, was 0.7. Despite *specifically* selecting issues on which their respective

---

[9] To measure the effect of corrections, we estimated linear models of the following form:

$$Agreement_i = f\!i_0 + f\!i_1(ideology) + f\!i_2(correction) + f\!i_3(ideology \times correction). \qquad (2.1)$$

Where i indexes issues. Agreement was measured on a five-point Likert scale, with larger values indicating stronger agreement. We measured ideology on a seven-point Likert scale, with larger values indicating increased conservatism. Corrections were measured with a dummy indicator. The choice of the OLS model and the specific measures for agreement, ideology, and correction were chosen to be consistent with Nyhan and Reifler (2010).

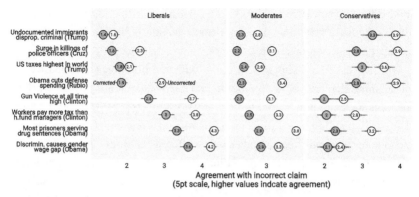

Figure 2.3 Regression estimates for expected values for Study 1 treatments, by correction and ideology. Light grey points and labels show the predicted level of agreement among uncorrected respondents, dark grey points among corrected respondents. Respondents' ideology is provided in the facet labels. Each issue is given on the y-axis, with corrected speakers inside parentheses. For each issue, larger values indicate agreement with an inaccurate statement. Error bars indicate 95 percent confidence intervals. Dark points remaining to the left of the light points indicate *improvement* in accuracy following correction.

leaders have drilled ideologues, a corrective statement achieves almost 70 percent of ideology's impact.[10]

Different Parties, Same Issues

We designed a second study to account for the possibility that the set of issues tested could drive respondents to become less accurate after corrections. We tested misstatements made by both parties that could be corrected by referring to the same data. Leaders from both parties have made erroneous claims about a number of issues. For example, Republican Senator (and then-presidential candidate) Ted Cruz falsely intimated that the number of illegal immigrants deported by President Obama was declining. On the same issue, Democratic Congressman Luis Gutierrez asserted that Obama was committed to reducing deportations. Cruz and Gutierrez had divergent motives for their misstatements, with Cruz wishing to portray Obama as unacceptably tolerant of illegal immigration, while Gutierrez aiming for the opposite. In both cases, this impression was inaccurate:

---

[10] Throughout the text, we describe corrections as prompting increases/decreases in factual accuracy. As a reviewer wisely pointed out, accuracy increases can be observed among subjects who never would fully "accept" the correction, and among those who would never "reject" it.

Department of Homeland Security data showed that Obama was deporting illegal immigrants at twice the rate of his predecessor.

We tested this and seven other bipartisan misconceptions. We randomly assigned subjects to see a misstatement by either a Democratic or Republican politician and then randomly exposed some to a correction. After seeing a misstatement and a correction (or not), all subjects were asked to agree with the position advanced by the misstatement, using the same five-point scale as before. For five of the eight corrections, we could point subjects to government data; for the remaining three, we simply asserted that the facts were not on the side of the politician. We again estimated the model specified in Equation 2.1. All misstatements appear in the online Appendix.

Figure 2.4 demonstrates that for none of the forty-eight combinations of respondent ideologies, speaker ideologies, and issues do we observe backfire or, indeed, even an *insignificant factual improvement*. Comparing correction effects within each issue row shows the extent of partisan motivated reasoning – that is, a tendency to be made more accurate by a correction if the correction allowed subjects to contradict a counter-partisan speaker. Table 2.1 summarizes these corrections, averaging across issues.

Consistent with the possibility that corrections are filtered via an ideological screen, with counter- partisan speakers readily contradicted and co-partisans reluctantly so, Table 2.1 demonstrates a preference for corrections to counter-partisans. However, for no cohort are the differences in correction effects statistically significant. Respondents do not seem systematically motivated to filter the corrections for ideological effect. Instead, the average correction effect on false beliefs was negative.

Table 2.1 Study 2 mean correction effects, by respondent and speaker ideologies, averaging over issues. Both liberal and conservative respondents are more responsive to corrections of their adversaries, but these differences are not significant. These estimates summarize the corrections depicted in Figure 2.4. Correction effects were measured on a five-point scale, with lower numbers corresponding to greater accuracy.

		Speaker Ideology	
		Liberal	Conservative
	Liberal	−1.10	−1.12
Subject Ideology	Moderate	−1.08	−1.06
	Conservative	−1.25	−1.13

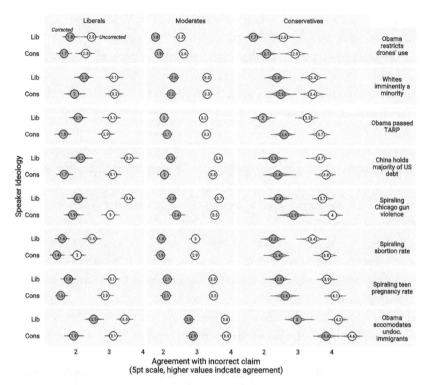

Figure 2.4 Regression estimates for expected values for Study 2 treatments, by correction and ideology. Light grey points and labels show the predicted level of agreement among uncorrected respondents, dark grey points among corrected respondents. Respondents' ideology is provided in the column facet labels. Each issue is labeled on the row facets – within each group, the liberal and conservative speakers are delineated on the y-axis. For each issue, larger values indicate agreement with an inaccurate statement. Error bars indicate 95 percent confidence intervals. Dark points remaining to the left of the light points indicate *improvement* in accuracy following correction.

Backfire in Newspaper Articles

By this stage in our study of backfire, we were flummoxed by our inability to induce the effect. Existing research – such as the original Nyhan and Reifler paper, in which backfire was observed on two-thirds of corrections – suggested that the effect was widespread, especially among issues of ideological import. We were struck by the stubborn refusal of our subjects to behave in the fashion we had expected.[11]

---

[11] Far from being theoretical iconoclasts, one of us was, to this point, an *acolyte* of backfire, and we were making every effort to induce the behavior in our subjects.

For a third study, we followed Nyhan and Reifler as closely as possible, with treatments hidden inside articles. We tested a mix of new and old issues. For example, we again leveraged Democratic politicians' embellishment of gun violence. For that issue, we inserted a misleading claim by President Obama into an article about gun violence in Chicago. "In my hometown of Chicago, gun violence and homicides have spiked – and in some cases they've spiked significantly. ... Because that's real, we've got to get on top of it before it becomes an accelerating trend," declared the president in an article entitled "Bloody Weekend in Chicago – 10 Killed, 53 Wounded in Violent Long Weekend." (Although this article had not actually appeared in a newspaper, it was modeled on such articles.) Obama's quote appeared at about the halfway point of the article. Those randomly assigned to read a version with a correction then saw the following: "Police department records, however, show a steady decline in homicides since the early 1990s, with 2014 having the fewest killings of any year since 1979."

We constructed six articles of roughly equal length that highlighted misstatements by politicians; for each article, we also created a version with a correction. As these treatments were meant to resemble actual articles, we included a plausible newspaper name (e.g., the aforementioned story about Chicago gun violence was said to come from *The Chicago Daily News*), a generic reporter's name (e.g., Laura McFarlane) and a date (e.g., July 5, 2015). As before, we then measured subjects' agreement with the factually incorrect claim made by the politician. In the Chicago gun violence article, we asked all subjects: "Do you agree or disagree with the following statement?" and provided them with a 1–5 agree/disagree scale: "Homicides in Chicago are currently at an all-time low."

Subjects were also shown a fictitious article originally used in Nyhan and Reifler's study. The article relayed President Bush's misleading claims about WMDs, while the correction pointed out that no WMDs had been found. However, we made one crucial modification. In the original study, Nyhan and Reifler measured backfire by asking subjects to agree with the following:

> Immediately before the U.S. invasion, Iraq had an active weapons of mass destruction program, the ability to produce these weapons, and large stockpiles of WMD, but Saddam Hussein was able to hide or destroy these weapons right before U.S. forces arrived (Nyhan and Reifler 2010).

To us, that measure seemed unwieldy. For the previous studies we had done, we'd asked subjects to agree with more succinct outcome measures. Following that approach, we randomly assigned subjects to see one of two WMD items – the Nyhan and Reifler item as shown or a simplification, which better tapped a subject's factual understanding:

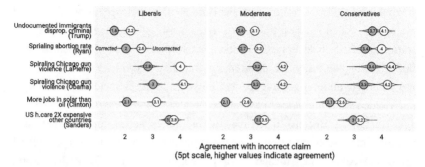

Figure 2.5 Regression estimates for expected values for Study 3 treatments, by correction and ideology. Light grey points and labels show the predicted level of agreement among uncorrected respondents, dark grey points among corrected respondents. Respondents' ideology is provided in the column facet labels. Each issue is labeled on the y-axis. For each issue, larger values indicate agreement with an inaccurate statement. Error bars indicate 95 percent confidence intervals. Dark points remaining to the left of the light points indicate *improvement* in accuracy following correction. Estimates that are significantly different from 0 (p < .05) are indicated by a thicker border.

> Following the US invasion of Iraq in 2003, US forces did not find weapons of mass destruction.

The results from this experiment are plotted in Figure 2.5. This figure shows that correction effects shrink when the treatments are embedded in a longer treatment – but still, we were unable to induce backfire. Of special interest was the comparison between the correction effects that followed the original Nyhan and Reifler survey item and the effects that followed our simpler item. These comparisons are depicted in Figure 2.6. Our item did see significant accuracy increases (among liberals), while the more complicated item compressed conditional differences.

Backfire and Survey Item Effects

While our comparatively less complex question did not yield backfire, it may be the case that more complex question wordings provoke respondents to counter-argue corrections. We designed Study 4 to test this possibility. We created three distinct outcomes statements for six issues. Each outcome statement varied in complexity, as subjects were asked their agreement with either a simple, moderately complex, or a complex statement. This resulted in eighteen outcome question wordings (six issues crossed with three levels of complexity). We embedded misleading claims and corrections in fictitious news articles. (The text of the articles is in the online Appendix.)

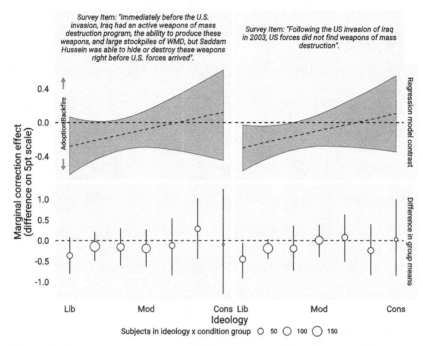

Figure 2.6 Regression correction effect estimates and simple group differences, by ideology and survey item, for Iraq-WMD correction. In the top row, each ribbon shows the 95 percent confidence interval for the correction effect (on a five-point scale). Positive values indicate degraded accuracy; negative values indicate otherwise. In the bottom row, we report the mean correction effects and their 95 percent confidence intervals, for every ideological cohort within each condition. The column facets indicate the experimentally assigned survey items – the left column shows correction effects for the original survey item, while the right column shows effects for our item.

For example, subjects read a news story in which Republican Congressman Paul Ryan falsely claimed that the abortion rate was increasing. Some were then randomly assigned to see a correction. All subjects were then asked to agree with *one of the following:*

Simple "The number of abortions performed in the US annually is at an all-time high."

Moderate "While the incidence of abortion is difficult to estimate because of privacy issues, the number of abortions in the US annually is at an all-time high."

Complex "While the incidence of abortion is difficult to estimate because of privacy issues, and also because of the threat that these numbers were

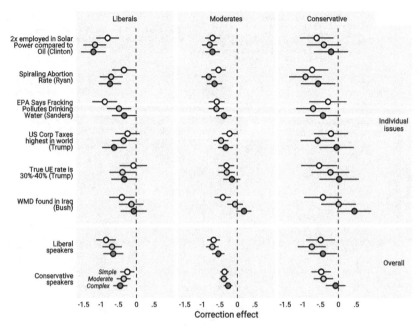

Figure 2.7 Regression correction effect estimates and their 95 percent confidence intervals, by treatment, ideology, and complexity of survey item. Each point range shows the estimated correction effect (on a five-point scale). Positive values indicate degraded accuracy; negative values indicate improved accuracy. The bottom facets average across the separate issues and group conservative speakers (Donald Trump, George Bush, and Paul Ryan) and liberal speakers (Hillary Clinton and Bernie Sanders).

changed for political reasons, the number of abortions in the US annually is at an all-time high."

Based on the discrepancy between our WMD finding as reported in Study 3 and Nyhan and Reifler's original finding, we expected that complex items would lead to backfire.[12] The most important correction estimates, by treatment, ideology, and item complexity, are depicted in Figure 2.7.

---

[12] This additional source of experimental variation requires a tweak to the model we've been using to measure corrections. In this model:

$$\text{Agreement}_i = fi_0 + fi_1 (\text{ideology} \times \text{correction} \times \text{complexity}) \qquad (2.2)$$

Complexity is a three-point categorical indicator, and ideology and corrections are measured as before (ideology as a continuous seven-point indicator, and corrections as a dichotomous indicator). The terms in Equation 2.2 expand to include thirteen coefficients, including two 3-way interactions.

Inspecting the bottom facets of Figure 2.7 demonstrates that complexity does not rescue backfire. Instead, it suggests that there might be a weak interaction between speaker ideology, respondent ideology, and item complexity: within each subject × ideology cohort, we see the strongest effect of complexity shrinking corrections' size when conservative subjects see conservative speakers corrected. We draw this connection cautiously, however, because of the small number of items we test in each experiment. Yet even here, our results do not correspond with the theoretical expectations of backfire, and we remained incapable of observing it.

Out of concern that our effects might have been driven by our use of Mechanical Turk, we hired Lucid, a provider of samples benchmarked to census data, to field a survey experiment replicating our previous findings. We simultaneously replicated our experiments on Mechanical Turk. While Mechanical Turk subjects were slightly more responsive to corrections, we failed to find backfire on Lucid; in almost all cases, the effects were indistinguishable across Turk and Lucid. Further discussion of this study can be found in "Backfire Replication Study" in the online Appendix.

Accordance between Misinformation and Corrections

Perhaps corrections that were substantively distant from their related misstatement would yield smaller correction effects than corrections that were more closely related to the misstatement. In the previous studies, we were limited by our decision to use only real-world misstatements and corrections. As others have noted, real-world corrections are often riddled with ambiguities and inconsistencies (e.g., Uscinski and Butler 2013).

To investigate, we had Mechanical Turk subjects evaluate all our misstatement/correction pairs as well as Nyhan and Reifler's. To make our objective clear, we told all the following:

> We're not asking if the statement is wrong, or if the correction is right. We're just asking how *closely related* they are. Is the factual correction above unrelated, partially related, or closely related to the political misstatement?

Above each misstatement and correction was a 0–100 slider that subjects could adjust to tell us whether the misstatement and correction were more or less proximate to each other. Did the corrections that subjects found to be more distantly related to the misstatement produce systematically different effects?

Our evidence suggests not. Figure 2.8 shows that average correction effects did not vary based on perceptions of how closely related corrections were to misstatements. Closely related misstatement-correction pairs and more distant pairs yielded about the same-size average effect. The advantage of our inclusive

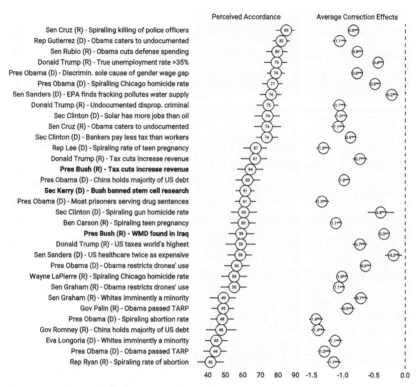

Figure 2.8 Perceived accordance between misstatement and correction pair and associated correction effect. The left panel reports accordance, while the right panel reports average correction effects. Accordance reports not how much a respondent is persuaded by a correction but how closely related they perceive the correction and the misstatement to be. The correction-misstatement pairs used in Nyhan and Reifler (2010) are in bold. In the online Appendix, we depict these same estimates in a more conventional scatterplot without labels.

Note: *** p < .001, ** p < .01, * p <.05

approach to treatments is demonstrated when contrasting our fifty-plus corrections to the three issues in the original backfire paper. The three Nyhan and Reifler issues fall in the middle of the scale; corrections are both far more and less accordant. Ultimately, there is no indication that accordance between misstatement and correction can account for our failure to find backfire.

The 2016 Election

While we had been testing the backfire effect, we had also inadvertently been testing Americans' factual receptivity during the 2016 election. Were misleading or false political statements during this time unusually capable of fostering

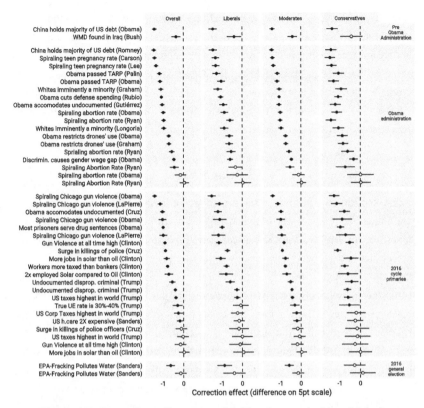

Figure 2.9 Correction effects organized by time period in which the misstatement was made and correction size. Hollow points indicate an insignificant correction. Overall effects average over the ideological cohorts. Labels repeat in the y-axis when the same issue was tested multiple times.

resistance to corrections? Figure 2.9 offers an answer. It displays all the correction effect sizes for the studies in this section, grouped by both the political period in which the initial statement was uttered and the size of the related correction effect. As we conducted these studies during both parties' primaries and through the general election, the top two panels of the figure display correction effects for those misstatements with the largest time difference between misstatement and test. When we look at overall correction effects, we see virtually all effects being significant and in the direction of greater accuracy across ideologies. While some effects were larger than others, the pattern was consistent.

These results might lead one to think that corrections can increase accuracy when the misstatement occurred some time ago. Yet as Figure 2.9 shows, even during the primaries, the majority of corrections elicited overall gains in accuracy. During this moment of heightened political contestation, liberals, conservatives, and moderates responded to corrections by becoming more accurate on average. Naturally, corrections to some issues generated larger effects than others. But again, throughout the 2016 presidential campaign, average subjects responded to corrections by becoming more accurate. If backfire describes a widespread reflex in the American public, the implications for democracy would be worrisome. Yet during this election, we repeatedly found the opposite – across the political spectrum, exposure to facts increased accuracy.

3 Fake News

In this section, we slightly alter the scope of our studies. Rather than just examining the relationship between misinformation, factual corrections, and factual receptivity, we look specifically at "fake news," investigating whether corrections to fake news can make people more accurate – and, if so, for how long. By one definition, "fake news" refers to "fabricated information that mimics news media content in form but not in organizational process or intent," produced by news outlets that "lack the news media's editorial norms and processes for ensuring the accuracy and credibility of information" (Lazer et al. 2018, p. 1094). This definition, however, hardly exhausts all on offer. One recent review of definitions of fake news within the published literature finds that scholars have used the term to refer to material that fits the rigid Lazer et al. (2018) definition but also manipulative advertising and propaganda (Tandoc et al. 2017), which runs outside the former.

Like concerns about the rise of post-truth politics, concerns about the proliferation of fake news are not new either. Such concerns, which seem to go part and parcel with an unregulated free press, date back to the republic's earliest days. "There has been more new error propagated by the press in the last ten years than in an hundred years before 1798," wrote President John Adams (Mansky 2018). This was an ironic conclusion, given that the American revolutionaries, of whom Adams was one, had circulated pamphlets filled with fictitious accounts of British atrocities. The *Boston Gazette* published stories alleging that British soldiers were routinely "beating children, forcing their attention on young ladies, [and] stealing merchandise from shopkeepers," not to mention violating the Sabbath (Burns 2006, p. 148). Almost all such accounts were fake – instances of colonial fake news.

What role did fake news play in the 2016 election, if any? During the 2016 election and shortly thereafter, many of the fake stories people encountered cast Trump in a favorable light. According to one fake story, Pope Francis had broken with all Vatican precedent and endorsed Trump's candidacy. According to another, Trump had personally paid to rescue stranded Marines. Yet another described Democratic campaign officials as enmeshed in an underground child sex ring. Still another alleged that Hillary Clinton had provided funding to ISIS.

In the three months preceding election day, Facebook users shared, reacted to, and commented on more fake stories than non-fake stories (Silverman 2016). Post-election survey results suggest that the average American could recall about 1.14 fake stories (Allcott and Gentzkow 2017). In the month before the election, about one in four Americans visited a fake news site (Guess, Nyhan, and Reifler 2018). While some fake stories favored Clinton, the majority were beneficial to Trump (Silverman 2016). Fake stories favoring Trump were shared 30 million times, while stories favoring Clinton were shared at little more than 25 percent of that (Allcott and Gentzkow 2017). Trump voters visited fake news sites far more often than Clinton voters. Moreover, about 40 percent of the former read a fake article from a pro-Trump site, while only 15 percent of Clinton voters did (Guess, Nyhan, and Reifler 2018). Thus, not only was fake news in wide circulation around the election, but fake news seemed to system-atically favor the winning candidate. Some evidence suggests that the public's appetite for fake news is unlikely to dissipate. An exhaustive study of Twitter concluded that at least on that platform, fake news spreads faster than non-fake news (Vosoughi, Roy, and Aral 2018).

On the one hand, it is tempting to review this evidence and despair. If people have a natural tendency to engage more with fake news than real news, what hope is there for citizens in a democracy? It would seem that people prefer the illusions of fake news to the humdrum realities of real news. On the other hand, decades of research in political communications suggest that the effects of political messaging are quite limited. While the public may imagine that media determines electoral outcomes, a paucity of evidence supports that claim (Mutz 2012). Especially in an age of extreme partisan polarization, people's minds are probably made up well before they encounter one fake news article – about the average amount consumed during the election (Allcott and Gentzkow 2017). Indeed, compared to previous years, Republican voters in 2016 were less likely to use the Internet than other groups, throwing more cold water on the idea that fake news was pivotal to the outcome (Boxell, Gentzkow, and Shapiro 2018).

Recall our motivating argument: subjects can pursue accuracy and partisan goals simultaneously. Upon encountering fake news that flatters their political affiliations, they may smile; however, upon seeing a correction to it, they may be content to be made more accurate, while retaining the affiliation that made them smile in the first place. Our evidence strongly supports this view. In our research, we have found that the average effect of corrections to fake news stories is consistently in the direction of increased accuracy across ideological and partisan groups. We tested fake stories that cast both sides in favorable lights; corrections made both sides more accurate. Some of the stories we tested had been in circulation for years; others were of more recent vintage. We tested different kinds of corrections. No matter the fake story, and no matter the correction method, the results were similar. On average, corrections to fake news increased accuracy.

Correcting Fake News

In summer 2017, we recruited a sample over Mechanical Turk. We tested six fake stories, randomly assigning subjects to see two stories each. For each story, we randomly provided some subjects with a correction. All subjects were then asked to state their agreement with the position advanced by the fake story. Because we wanted to know if one ideological or partisan group was more resistant than the other to correction, we strove to identify fake news examples from both sides. Theoretically, each one of the fake stories we tested could have proven resistant to correction by the ideological group that the story flattered.

In several treatments, we have deviated from the strict Lazer et al. (2018) definition of fake news. While those authors describe fake news as emanating from an "organizational process or intent" that mimics but is fundamentally distinct from traditional media content, we tested several stories that came from traditional media processes but were shown to be fraudulent. For example, we tested a story in which *ABC News*'s Brian Ross claimed that during the presidential campaign, Trump directed Michael Flynn to make contact with the Russian government. Soon after airing, this story was found to be inaccurate and was retracted. The story had followed, for the most part, the standard process to publication at traditional media outlets. We included it in our tests nonetheless. From the perspective of a news consumer, the process that precedes publication is invisible. Ultimately, if a story advances wildly erroneous information, it is fundamentally "fake," regardless of the publication process that preceded it.

Choosing Fake News Stories

We tested fake stories that flattered conservatives and denigrated liberals. We tested a story accusing "top Democrat John Podesta" of overseeing a pedophile ring from the basement of a Washington, DC–based pizza parlor – a story known as "Pizzagate." We also tested a story alleging that "top Democrats John and Tony Podesta" may have been involved in the abduction of a European girl. Especially flattering to Trump supporters, we also tested a story crediting Trump for ordering the arrest "of an unprecedented number of sexual predators." Finally, we tested an oldie-but-goodie: the claim that Barack Obama was not actually born in the United States. (The full text of all the fake stories and attendant corrections appear in the online Appendix.)

The leak of Clinton campaign chairman John Podesta's email account offered much fodder to fake news purveyors. Perhaps the most famous fake story involving Podesta was the Pizzagate story. In brief, the claim was that when properly decoded, the leaked emails make clear that Podesta was in charge of a pedophile ring for Democrats, run out of a Comet Ping Pong, a pizza restaurant – hence the name "Pizzagate." Of course, there was no truth to any of this.

To test the effects of corrections on beliefs about Pizzagate, we presented subjects with a description of the conspiracy that had proliferated on conservative message boards and websites. Consisting of multiple "exhibits," the story rests on claims such as "Comet's logo ... resembles a pedophile symbol" and that there were references in Podesta's emails to Comet Ping Pong, children, and maps on handkerchiefs. ("In the gay community," the story helpfully explains, "handkerchiefs are sometimes used as code for sexual preferences.")

After the Pizzagate story, subjects randomly assigned to read a correction were directed to a correction consisting of a story by Snopes.com, the popular fact-checking website. After declaring the story to be false, the correction reviews the entire story that respondents had just read. Then, the correction explains that the fake story is actually a heap of coincidences dressed up into something coherent. Finally, all subjects were asked to agree or disagree with the following statement: "High-ranking Democrat John Podesta was involved in a pedophile ring at a pizza parlor." Responses could be given on a five-point scale.

We also tested a fake story that alleged that John Podesta, as well as his brother Tony Podesta, also a well-known Democratic operative, may have been involved in the abduction of a seven-year-old girl in Portugal. As this fake story rested on the claim that "the brothers resemble the police sketch artist's portrait of the suspected kidnappers," we presented subjects with pictures of the brothers and the police sketch in question. Again, the fake news example used here is real; the image we tested had circulated widely. For a correction, we again relied on Snopes.com, which explains (as is so often the case), "Context is key." In this case," The sketch depicts not two but one man, and that man was sought as a witness to the kidnapping (not necessarily a perpetrator of or accessory to it)." All subjects were asked to agree with the following: "Top Democrats John and Tony Podesta may have been involved in an abduction."

We tested a story that we thought would have immense appeal to Trump supporters. The claim that President Trump was responsible for ordering a large-scale, national crackdown on sex crimes was not relegated to the

Internet fringes. Indeed, the version of the fake story we tested came from Townhall.com, a well-known conservative site. The article in question, "Why the MSM Is Ignoring Trump's Sex Trafficking Busts," asserted that a "staggering 1,500-plus arrests [of pedophiles] in one short month" was attributable to Trump.

For a correction, we used an article from *Reason*, a libertarian magazine. As the corrective article pointed out, many of the arrests described as part of Trump's crackdown on sex crimes had, in fact, nothing to do with sex crimes. Moreover, many of the arrests made were owed to investigations that began long before Trump's presidency. This fake story imbued Trump with powers he did not have, giving him credit for law enforcement decisions that he did not make. On the same scale as before, we asked all subjects to agree with the proposition of the fake story.

Finally, we turned to Obama's birth certificate. Few fake stories have received as much attention as this one; Trump himself had made political hay of it before running for president. To present the story, we directed participants to a YouTube video of a news clip in which a law enforcement official explained that his office was investigating the veracity of the birth certificate.

Rather than point subjects to a Snopes.com article, we showed subjects assigned to treatment a photo of Obama's birth announcement as it originally appeared in a Hawaii newspaper. "Here is what Barack Obama's birth announcement looked like in the Obamas' local Hawaii newspaper," read the text, with a picture of the announcement below. All subjects told us whether they agreed with the declaration that "Barack Obama was born in Hawaii." No other information was provided.

In choosing fake stories to test that might appeal to liberals, we adopted an expansive definition of fake news. While Allcott and Gentzkow (2017) rule out retracted news stories from their fake news analysis, we decided to include them nonetheless. We did so for several reasons. First, as noted previously, from the perspective of participants not assigned to control – that is, subjects who did not receive a correction – these stories were no different from other fake stories. They offered political information that favored one side over another; this information, however, had little relationship to the truth. Second, both of the stories we tested were widely discussed prior to being retracted. Retractions typically have less persuasive power than initial stories (Berinsky 2017). Third, unlike the aforementioned conservative stories, the retracted liberal stories were originally published in well-known outlets. Source effects may have explained the results we observed for conservative stories, with subjects rejecting stories not because they were fake but because they were not advanced by credible sources. Finally, the liberal stories we tested were subjected to fact-checks like the conservative ones we tested, facilitating the comparison of effect sizes across ideological groups.

One fake story we tested latched onto post-election liberal anxiety about the extent of Russian infiltration in the United States. "Russian Hackers Penetrated U.S. Electricity Grid through a Utility in Vermont, Officials Say," read the headline in the *Washington Post* on the last day of 2016. The article alleged that "a code" associated with Russia had been found in the Vermont power grid. In short order, however, it was revealed that crucial components of the story were false. Three days later, the same journalists published a story with a much different headline: "Russian Government Hackers Do Not Appear to Have Targeted Vermont Utility, Say People Close to Investigation." It turned out that the IP address that was found to have visited one electric company employee's laptop – the IP address that sparked initial suspicions – was not affiliated with Russian hackers. Furthermore, the laptop itself was not actually connected to the power grid. All this was explained in the corrective article.

For this fake story, we also varied the correction that treatment subjects would see. Some saw the *Washington Post*'s own correction. Others were assigned to read a different article. "Russia Hysteria Infects WashPost Again: False Story About Hacking U.S. Electric Grid," proclaimed *The Intercept*'s Glenn Greenwald. Greenwald, a critic of claims about Russia's role in the 2016 election, not only documented the erroneous claims in the *Post*'s piece but also connected the piece to a larger trend of liberal embellishments about Russia. "The social media benefits from tweeting and publishing unhinged claims about Trump and Putin are immense," he wrote. All subjects who read a story and/or a correction about Vermont responded to: "The Russian government infiltrated Vermont's power grid."

Even if they were moved by the *Washington Post*'s follow-up article to become more accurate, we might have expected liberals to *not* become more accurate after viewing the Greenwald article. While the substance of the corrective material was similar, Greenwald's tone was sharper; as the previous quote shows, his corrective article was broader, calling into question other liberal concerns about Trump. A liberal who responded to Greenwald's correction by becoming more accurate would have to do so even though she would be experiencing cross-pressure against her ideological affiliations.

We tested another fake story that might bait liberals into rejecting corrections. This article, "Congress Investigating Russian investment Fund with Ties to Trump Officials," was published by CNN in June 2017. The article reported that the Senate was investigating then-Trump adviser Anthony Scaramucci for connections to a fund controlled by Russia and promises to lift sanctions.

Those who saw a correction were then directed to a *New York Times* article that described the fallout: CNN had not only retracted the story and apologized for publishing it, but the journalists who wrote it had resigned in disgrace. "Fake news!" Trump tweeted in response to the retraction – a tweet the *Times* article highlighted, and that subjects in both conditions saw. If liberals were to respond to the correction by becoming more accurate, they would have to do so at the expense of implicitly agreeing with Trump.

Results

That's exactly what they did. In response to a question that read, "The Senate is currently investigating a meeting between Trump adviser Anthony Scaramucci and the Russia Direct Investment Fund," subjects who saw the correction – including liberals – were more accurate. On average, across all conditions, subjects were made more accurate by corrections of fake news.

Figure 3.1 displays results. On a five-point scale in which smaller numbers indicate less agreement with the fake story, correction effects ranged from −.3 to 1.06 – all substantively large and statistically significant. The smallest effect was observed on the Obama birth certificate story; this may be explained by how long that story had been in circulation, which likely placed a ceiling on any effects. But even then, we still found that a parsimonious correction – just *showing* people Obama's birth announcement – could increase accuracy. The largest correction effect, meanwhile, was observed on the correction for the retracted *Washington Post* article about Russia hacking Vermont's power grid, a story that had only recently begun to circulate.

For that story, it didn't matter what kind of correction subjects saw: the verbose, normatively laden Greenwald correction was just as effective at increasing accuracy as the neutral *Washington Post* correction. When we take subjects' ideology into account, the Greenwald correction was actually more powerful at convincing respondents to become more accurate. This was true of ideologues from both sides. Conservatives who viewed the Greenwald correction moved −1.05 on our outcome variable, while conservatives who saw the *Post*'s correction moved −.81. Similarly, liberals who saw the Greenwald correction moved −1.17, while liberals who saw the *Post*'s moved −1.06.

For all stories, we observed correction effects in the direction of the more accurate position cross ideologies. Figure 3.1 makes this clear. Take, for example, the fake story describing Trump as overseeing a vast crackdown on pedophilia. Liberals exposed to a correction became more accurate on average, but so too did conservatives. Or consider the story about Scaramucci and Russia. Again, we observed average correction effects in the direction of greater

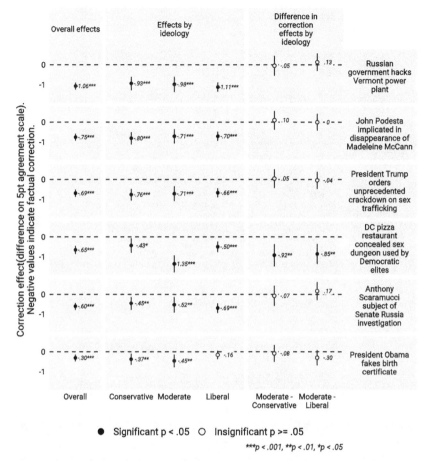

Figure 3.1 Correction effects for the fake news stories. The first column reports overall corrections, the second reports corrections among ideological cohorts, and the third reports differences between the ideological cohorts. Point ranges indicate 95 percent confidence intervals.

accuracy for conservatives, as one might expect, but we saw liberals doing the same. (Result tables for this study can be found in the online Appendix.)

Do Corrective Effects Last?

In our previous studies, we showed participants an example of misinformation or fake news; then showed some of them a correction; and, finally, measured their factual beliefs. While this design mirrors that of previous research into factual receptivity (e.g., Kuklinski 2000; Nyhan and Reifler 2010), it leaves open the question of whether corrections stick. It may be that immediately after seeing a correction, subjects are, on average, more accurate – but that the effects

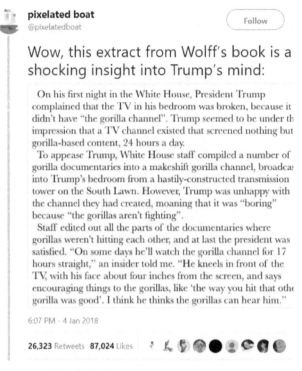

Figure 3.2 The gorilla channel story

fade, as people snap back to their partisan prior beliefs. Do correction effects last?

We administered an experiment to answer. Here's how it worked. In the spring of 2018, we followed our standard procedure, recruiting people over Mechanical Turk, showing all subjects examples of fake news, showing some of them corrections, and then measuring effects. Over the following month, we recontacted all subjects and asked them to again tell us their level of belief in the fake news item that they had seen. To avoid confounding our estimates by response date, we recontacted a random subset of our subjects every day and directed them to the survey. This left us with two effects to measure: the immediate effects of seeing a correction and the effects measured days, weeks, and even a month later.[13]

We used some of the fake news examples used in the previous study, while adding a few new ones. Once again, we tested the claim that Trump had

---

[13] The operating assumption of this study is that all subjects are either "Always-Reporters" or "Never-Reporters," with the randomized timing of assignment to receive a posttreatment survey constituting the only difference between subjects. For further discussion, consult Gerber and Green (2012).

overseen an "unprecedented" crackdown on sex crimes and the Pizzagate story. (The online Appendix contains the outcome variables and the full text of the treatments or, given fair use restrictions, links for where they may be found.) We also tested a story that alleged that the Trump administration had left LGBT and black reporters off the invite lists for White House Christmas parties. To correct respondents, we showed an excerpt of a fact-check attributed to Snopes.com. The verdict of this fact-check was ambiguous, however. "Since we were unable to confirm who was on the guest list because the White House would not respond to our questions, and a Freedom of Information request for that information has not yet been responded to, we cannot support the claim that guests were excluded because of their race or sexual preference," it read.

We again relied on existing journalistic corrections to erroneous published stories. In this study, we showed some participants a clip of *ABC News*'s Brian Ross, in which Ross claimed that former Trump national security adviser Michael Flynn would testify that Trump had directed Flynn to "make contact with the Russians" during the election. For a correction, we showed a clip of Ross himself disavowing the story. The Ross story was so egregious that Trump had the GOP award Ross a "fake news of the year" award. At random, we showed some respondents that information – Trump's "award" to Ross – as well, reasoning that this would offer liberals more reason to counter-argue and be made less accurate by the correction. We asked all subjects if they agreed that Trump had ordered Flynn to make contact "during the election."

We also tested a claim that Hillary Clinton had exchanged uranium for donations to the Clinton Foundation by Russia. We showed respondents an ominous campaign video making the accusation – a video produced by Trump's campaign. Our inclusion of this advertisement in a test of fake news is consistent with other work that regards political propaganda as fake news (e.g., Khaldarova and Pantti 2016). In our study, respondents assigned to a correction saw an article that made clear Clinton did not have authority to give the Russians uranium and thus could not have participated in a quid pro quo deal with the Russian government. We asked subjects if they agreed with the following: "In 2010, then-Secretary of State Hillary Clinton approved the sale of US uranium to Russia in return for payments to the Clinton Foundation." As the correction made clear, this claim was false.

Our final fake story was rather humorous. In the wake of *Fire and Fury*, Michael Wolff's tome about Trump's first year in office, various fake stories cropped up that claimed to be from the book but were actually made up. We tested a tweet that purported to be an excerpt from the book, focusing on Trump's television habits. According to the tweet, Trump spent upward of seventeen hours a day watching "gorilla- based content," via a television

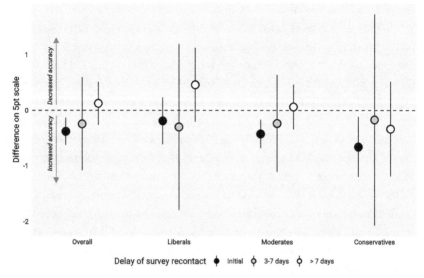

Figure 3.3 Attenuation study results. Each point range shows the average correction effect, and its 95 percent confidence interval, according to respondent ideology, and the delay before a subject was invited to complete a follow-up. Point ranges average of the separate corrected issues.

channel his staff had curated personally for him. We showed everyone who saw this fake item a correction from Pundifact.[14]

As we lack strong theoretical priors about each specific fake news item, we analyze our results by collapsing across items. Figure 3.3 illustrates our results for all subjects and when conditioning on ideology. Rather than attending to the minor differences in recontact time, we place responses into three groups: those gathered immediately after treatment, those gathered three to seven days later, and those gathered more than seven days later.

For all subjects, and virtually every ideological group, a pattern appears: while corrections were able to increase accuracy at first, the effects became smaller over time. Across items, correction effects were not statistically

---

[14] Specifically, on a one-to-five scale, with higher numbers indicating increased agreement, in this study we directed all subjects to do the following: "For each statement below, please indicate how strongly you disagree or agree." We then presented the following statements: "The Trump White House banned black and LGBT reporters from their Christmas party"; "At President Trump's direction, White House staff made a TV channel which exclusively depicted gorillas fighting"; "President Trump is leading an unprecedented effort to increase the number of arrests for sex trafficking"; "High-ranking Democrat John Podesta was involved in a pedophile ring at a pizza parlor"; "During the 2016 presidential campaign, Donald Trump ordered his adviser, retired General Michael Flynn, to make contact with Russia"; "In 2010, then-Secretary of State Hillary Clinton approved the sale of US uranium to Russia in return for payments to the Clinton Foundation."

distinguishable from zero after three days. Broadly speaking, as Figure 3.3 makes clear, correction effects dissipate quickly. A results table, with results for each fake item, can be found in the online Appendix. While correction effects were still detectable at the latest stage on one item, they were not on others.

While the passage of time did not lead subjects to backfire, we do not have evidence that corrections to fake news produce enduring accuracy increases. Carpini and Keeter (1996, pp. 11) write that the measurement of political knowledge should focus on what people know about politics in the long term, not "information that is never cognized or that is used in short-term memory but then discarded." From this perspective, our study shows that single corrections do not meaningfully increase political knowledge, in that they do not appear to endure for very long in subjects' memories. It may be that for subjects to remain accurate over time, they must see repeated corrections, also over time, to the same story.

At the least, across items, it is *not* the case that the average subject came to *believe* the initial fake story more than seven days after corrections. But for most items, the initial accuracy gains were gone. The initial misinformation was no longer affecting views, as the continued influence effect would predict, but neither were the subsequent corrections.

Implications

For the private and public sectors alike, fake news rightly constitutes a major concern – and rightly so. A small industry now exists to pollute the public with fraudulent stories. Major media companies sometimes show little interest in fact-checking their own stories, especially when those stories relate to major national controversies such as Russian meddling in American affairs. During recent Brazilian elections, journalists wrote about fake news circulating widely over WhatsApp, a chat application owned by Facebook (Isaac and Roose 2018). In 2018, the *New York Times* reported that the Myanmar military had been spreading fake news over Facebook for more than a decade as part of its ethnic cleansing campaign against the Rohingya population (Mozur 2018).

Yet we have repeatedly shown corrections targeted at fake news can increase accuracy. This is true regardless of the relationship between individuals' political preferences and the slant of the story. Our findings suggest that retractions can be just as powerful as formal corrections. However novel and alluring the fake examples we tested were, people generally responded to corrections by becoming more accurate. Fake news offers fabrications designed for partisans. Attesting to the dual-processing capabilities of average citizens, many of these same partisans become more accurate after a correction. However, we have little evidence that accuracy gains caused by corrections to fake news endure very long. Broadly speaking, this finding is consistent with our theoretical expectations. People do not care enough about facts to engage in motivated reasoning against them; however, because they care so little, the accuracy increases are fleeting.

For accuracy increases to be maintained, it may be necessary to repeatedly expose people to corrections. This will be difficult. There is strong evidence that people who consume fake news virtually never consume corrections (Guess, Nyhan, and Reifler 2018). The apparent mismatch between consumers of fake news and consumers of corrections helps explain the continuing existence of the fake news industry. Media outlets should not shy away from issuing corrections. As we have shown repeatedly, *at worst* corrections are ignored; more frequently, however, they result in a more accurate population, at least for a time. But more effort must be paid to alerting consumers of fake news to the existence of corrective information. It is not enough for media outlets to just publish fact-checks; if they aim to fight fake news, they must do more to persuade consumers of fake news to read fact-checks of the fake news they've read. One correction will likely not be enough. If media companies make such efforts, our research offers evidence that, on average, people will become more accurate.

4 Is Trump Different?

The evidence presented so far portrays people as generally responding to corrections of misinformation by becoming more accurate, even when the corrections cut against misstatements made by politicians from their preferred party or side of the ideological spectrum. Yet perhaps President Trump inspires a different response. If anyone would have the ability to convince people to reject corrective information, it would probably be this president. In the experiments we conducted during the 2016 campaign, we observed some of the smallest correction effects on misstatements made by then-candidate Trump. Does Trump have an unusual knack for not only uttering mistruths but also for convincing people to disregard corrections?

This section investigates Trump's capacity to sow misinformation. The stakes here are at once more specific, in that they investigate responses to one politician's misleading statements – but also more dire. More than anything, it has been Trump's seemingly unrepentant attitude toward spewing misstatements that has led scholars to declare American politics in crisis. Philosopher Jason Stanley, for example, has argued that Trump's repeated falsehoods make him a fascist politician (Stanley 2018). Stanley's diagnosis follows in the footsteps of historian Timothy Snyder, who, in after Trump's election, asserted that Trump's disregard for truth portended the rise of fascism. "Post-truth is pre-fascism," declared Snyder (2017, p. 71).

Politicians deviating from the truth are hardly a new phenomenon (e.g., Arendt 1971). Yet while many politicians mislead, Trump still stands out. By one measure, in his first year and a half as president, Trump made more than 3,000 false claims (Kessler, Rizzo, and Kelly 2018). His misstatements may be essential to his success. Hahl and colleagues (2018) marshal evidence about hypothetical political candidates to conclude that in times of perceived legitimacy crises, politicians can be seen as more "authentic" when they lie, with their lies constituting a form of "symbolic protest" (Hahl, Kim, and Sivan 2018, p. 24). They argue that their results help explain Trump's appeal. His constant lies "made him even more credible as an authentic champion of his supporters – mainly Americans who also felt disrespected by cultural elites" (Hahl, Kim, and Sivan 2018, pp. 24–25).

In this section, we present studies focused on Trump's misstatements. First, we consider a claim about crime he made during the 2016 Republican National Convention. Then, we look at a claim he made about unemployment during the first presidential debate. Next, we study claims he has made as president about climate change. We then test an editorial, riddled with falsifications, that he published on the eve of the 2018 election. We also investigate his 2019 State of the Union address.

When confronted with a correction to a Trump misstatement, in most cases, the average subject moves toward the accurate position. This has tended to be the case among Trump's supporters. When shown corrections to Trump's misstatements on crime, unemployment, the environment, and immigration, his supporters have, on average, become more accurate. This was even the case among conservatives who saw a correction to a Trump misstatement about immigration on the night of his 2019 State of the Union. This doesn't mean that his supporters become any less supportive of him because of one correction. When he misleads on a certain policy issue, being made more accurate by a correction does not impact Trump supporters' views on that issue. In general, Trump supporters respond to corrections by becoming more accurate, but their attitudes are unmoved.

Unsurprisingly, Trump does have strong influence over his co-partisans' attitudes. In another study, we isolate the ability of Trump as president to convince people to become more inaccurate. We do so by manipulating an editorial Trump published in *USA Today* on the eve of the 2018 election that was immediately decried by fact-checkers for advancing a litany of untruths. We randomly showed some subjects the editorial so that authorship would be attributed to Mitch McConnell, Republican Senate leader, instead of Trump. We observed larger effects in the direction of accuracy for McConnell than for Trump. However, the average Republican who saw a correction when authorship was attributed to Trump *did not* become less factually accurate. Republicans' responses to corrections do not translate into changes of their broader political views. During the campaign, exposure to corrections did not affect his supporters' approval ratings of him. During his presidency, exposure to a correction about a policy issue did not affect his supporters' views about that policy.

Another study presented here looks at the effects of misinformation and corrections on voters' approval of Trump. Two years into his presidency, we varied the "dosage" levels of his misstatements and corrections, evaluating effects on approval. We found some evidence that a larger number of Trump misstatements, unaccompanied by corrections, can increase approval – but when those same misstatements are followed by corrections, his approval declines in equal measure.

The RNC Study

During the 2016 campaign, we conducted a study meant to tease out how voters responded to factual corrections to Trump's RNC speech, and to his campaign's attempt to denigrate the fact-checkers. We conducted the study with Brendan Nyhan and Jason Reifler, the academics whose initial work on backfire in 2010 had inspired our own work (and who stand out as models of open-minded, rigorous researchers). In his speech, Trump made a set of hyperbolic claims about the crime rate in America. He declared there was an "epidemic" of violent crime in the United States. "In this race for the White House," he said, "I am the law and order candidate." Similar to the studies in Section 2, we created fictitious news articles, modeled on actual articles, and included Trump's statements in the articles. We also created an article with the following correction: "According to FBI's Bureau of Justice Statistics, the violent crime rate has fallen dramatically and consistently over time. According to their estimates, the homicide rate in the U.S. in 2015 was half that recorded in 1991."

Here was the twist. We also created articles meant to highlight how the campaign rejected the fact-checking that journalists applied to Trump's misstatement. Some subjects read an article that, in addition to the statement and correction, included a response by Paul Manafort, then Trump's campaign manager. "People don't feel safe in their neighborhoods," said Manafort, before going on to question the statistics underpinning the fact-check. We included that quote in one of our articles. We also created an article in which we further quoted Manafort. "The FBI is certainly suspect these days after what they just did with Hillary Clinton," Manafort said, referring to the non-prosecution of Clinton over the email scandal. We also had some subjects read a placebo article about a dog show. (The full text of all articles appears in the online Appendix.) After they read their article, we asked subjects a question meant to tease out their factual receptivity, another about their favorability toward the candidates, and a third about their feelings about the article they had just read.[15]

In sum, in addition to a conventional correction treatment, we tested treatments that featured Trump's campaign manager denigrating the data behind the correction, and one in which the campaign manager attributed a political motive to the data. Certainly for Trump supporters in that last condition, we reasoned, there would be enough material for them to respond to the correction by becoming less accurate. As a treatment condition, it was designed to maximize the probability that we would observe partisan allegiance triumphing over empirical evidence.[16]

In addition to relying on Mechanical Turk for survey recruitment, we also used a sample provided by Morning Consult, an online survey firm. Morning Consult uses post-stratification on data collected via opt- in online polls to produce data that approximates national representativeness. We worked with Morning Consult because we worried that our repeated success at avoiding backfire in previous studies was owed to the unusual nature of Mechanical Turk. The results we observed with the Lucid sample referred to in the Section 2 had reduced, though not eliminated, such concerns.

We administered the experiment on Mechanical Turk and Morning Consult samples simultaneously. We observed startlingly similar results on both. Note that we did not weight Mechanical Turk respondents in any way to mirror the greater representativeness of Morning Consult. Each treatment condition with a factual correction, including those in which Trump surrogates denigrated the correction, increased subjects' accuracy. Even those conditions in which we highlighted Trump surrogates' attacks on the correction *increased* accuracy. On

---

[15] Specifically, to measure factual receptivity, we asked: "Would you say that, compared to ten years ago, the violent crime rate has gone up, stayed about the same, or gone down?" Possible answers were "Gone up," "Stayed about the same," or "Gone down." If respondents replied that crime had gone up, we then asked: "Compared to ten years ago, has the violent crime rate gone up a lot or only somewhat?" They could respond with "Gone up a lot" or "Gone up somewhat." Alternatively, if respondents replied that crime had gone down, we asked: "Compared to ten years ago, has the violent crime rate gone down a lot or only somewhat?" and presented them with the choices "Gone down a lot" or "Gone down somewhat."

[16] Additional details on this experiment can be located in Nyhan, Porter, Reifler, and Wood (2017).

this five-point scale, in which smaller numbers corresponded to greater accuracy, correction effects on Turk and Consult ranged from $-.74$ to 1.12. A table of results appear in the online Appendix.

To be sure, in both samples Trump supporters were made less accurate by the correction than were Clinton supporters. This is consistent with what motivated reasoning would lead us to expect. However, when we difference Trump-supporting subjects who saw the conditions in which the correction was denigrated from Trump supporters who saw no correction, we still see large and significant movement toward accuracy.

Corrections did not affect how voters evaluated the candidates. Whether or not they saw a correction, Trump supporters remained supporters. On this five-point scale, with higher numbers corresponding to more positive views, almost no condition had any effect when we average across the sample and when we look at each candidate's supporters. A results table can be found in the online Appendix. The one exception was observed on Mechanical Turk, with subjects who saw just the fact-check condition becoming marginally less favorable toward Trump. But the effect was small and statistically ambiguous. On the whole, corrections can increase accuracy, even when supporters of the targeted politician are given reason by co-partisans to doubt the correction. But at least during a presidential election, corrections have limited power to affect political views.

The Debate Study

In the previous studies, there had been a lag between a misstatement and our measurement of correction effects. This presents several potential problems. It is possible that we've been exposing people to corrections about misstatements they do not have much invested in, making increasing accuracy a less costly exercise. On the other hand, it is also possible that people are less likely to be made accurate by a correction in the heat of the political moment, when partisan loyalties are at their apex. The design of our studies may have been leading us to underestimate or overestimate the extent to which corrections increase accuracy.

With such concerns in mind, we conducted a study on the night of the first debate between Trump and Clinton. Using Mechanical Turk, a week before the study we gathered basic demographic and political information on subjects and asked if they would have access to television on the night of the debate (without referring to the debate itself). After eliminating subjects who said they wouldn't be able to watch television that night, we randomly encouraged some to watch the debate, paying them to complete a survey after it was over and entering them into a raffle for more money. We told subjects that we would email them a link to a survey shortly after the debate ended.[17]

Early in the debate, Trump made a statement about unemployment in the United States, with references to "thousands of jobs leaving" Michigan and Ohio, implying that unemployment was on the upswing in both states. As fact-checkers working for National Public Radio and the *New York Times* pointed out during the debate, this was inaccurate. The *Times* reported the number of new jobs created in both states over the previous year (New York Times 2016), while NPR directed readers to Bureau of Labor Statistics data (National Public Radio 2016). At the very end of the survey, we sent to subjects shortly after the debate concluded, we presented all participants with this Trump claim:

> Our jobs are fleeing the country to Mexico … they're building some of the biggest, most sophisticated plants. Not so much in America. Thousands of jobs leaving Michigan, Ohio … their companies are just leaving, they're gone.[18]

Then, those randomly assigned to see a correction saw: "In fact, according to the Bureau of Labor Statistics, unemployment has fallen in both states. Both states each saw 70,000 new jobs over the last year." Our correction strongly echoed the corrections put out by fact-checkers at the same time. Like NPR's fact-checker, we relied on the Bureau of Labor Statistics to rebut Trump's claims. Like the *New York Times*, we showed participants the numbers of new jobs created in both states. Participants in our experiment who were assigned to treatment were seeing a fact-check that they could have plausibly seen on the night of the debate, thereby enhancing our external validity.

We then asked all participants to answer: "Over the last few years, has unemployment gone up or down in Michigan and Ohio?" On a five-point scale, available responses ranged from "Gone down a lot" to "Gone up a lot." Because we wanted to measure effects with the debate still fresh in memory, we stopped accepting responses the next morning. If Trump-supporting respondents wished to side with the candidate of choice on the night he was engaged in public combat with his opponent, they could have easily distanced themselves from the correction and evinced greater inaccuracy.

That is not what happened. Instead, on the night of the debate, the average participant – including the average Trump supporter – responded to the correction by becoming more accurate. For all participants, being assigned to

---

[17] This study was part of a broader study about cable news, discussed in Gross, Porter, and Wood (2018). Random assignment for that study was entirely separate from assignment for this study and had no bearing on these results.

[18] The survey was prepared before transcripts were available, so the statement in our study differs slightly from the official transcript.

a correction caused a .34 decrease on our five-point scale (in which smaller numbers corresponded to the factually accurate response). When we difference the responses of those who saw the fact-check from those who did not, we find that the effect size was *greater* for Trump's supporters than for Clinton's – again, with the effect being in the direction of increased accuracy. (Regression results appear in the online Appendix.)

The Climate Change Studies

Has President Trump proved better at persuading Americans to believe inaccuracies than candidate Trump? To answer, we looked at statements he has made as president about climate change.

First, we looked at a claim that Trump made about global warming and trends related to ice caps. He said that global warming "wasn't working out too well, because it was getting too cold all over the place. The ice caps were going to melt, they were going to be gone by now, but now they're setting records … they're at a record level." This claim was soon corrected by prominent fact-checkers (e.g., Greenberg 2018). Subjects who were assigned to receive a correction were told the following:

> In fact, according to NASA, this is incorrect. Polar ice caps are at record lows. They are the smallest they've been since satellite measurements began in 1979. They've shrunk by over 380,000 square miles since 2000, an 8% reduction in size.

Given the mass public's well-known difficulties with numeracy (e.g., Merola and Hitt 2016), this was a demanding correction. We then asked all subjects to rate their level of agreement with the statement that "The polar ice caps are at record low levels." Responses could be given on a five-point scale.[19]

We wanted to break away from the Internet-based samples we'd used for the previous studies. We partnered with Babak Bahador, a researcher with experience in administering phone surveys. We deployed climate change experiments simultaneously on Mechanical Turk and a random set of Americans reached over the telephone. Given our focus on how Trump voters reacted to corrections of Trump, reaching voters through the phone was especially helpful. In the United States, only landlines can receive unsolicited surveys; phone-only survey samples are therefore likely to skew older than Internet-based samples. Not only are Trump voters older than non-Trump voters, but older voters may also be more susceptible to misinformation than younger voters (Boxell,

---

[19] Specifically, subjects were asked: "Do you agree or disagree with the following statement: The polar ice caps are at record low levels."

Gentzkow, and Shapiro 2018; Guess, Tucker, and Nadler 2018). Insofar as we always designed our studies with an eye toward maximizing the probability of observing backfire, running a survey experiment over the phone should have helped our cause.

Correction effects by party for this question appear in Figure 4.1. The figure accounts for subjects reached via Mechanical Turk and telephone. The standard correction effect estimates can be glimpsed in the center panel. Upon seeing – or, in the case of our telephone subjects, hearing – a correction, average accuracy increased. Republicans, meanwhile, proved indifferent to the correction. Such respondents, however, did not become less accurate by the correction.

For the second climate change study, we presented different subjects with a different Trump misstatement. When he announced the United States was pulling out of the Paris Climate Accords, he asserted that the agreement

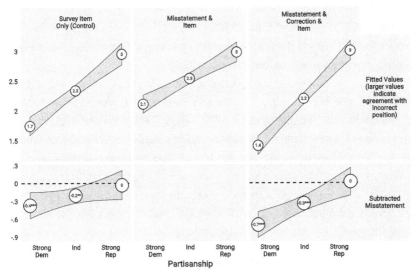

Figure 4.1 Correction effects about size of polar ice caps. The top row reports fitted values, and their associated 95 percent confidence intervals for models predicting agreement with Trump's claim about the size of the polar ice caps, as a function of respondent partisanship (on the x-axis), and their treatment conditions (in the columns). Larger values indicate more agreement with the incorrect claim – that polar ice caps are historically large. The next row reports contrasts between the fitted regression values – specifically, it subtracts the fitted value of those respondents who saw the misstatement. The area below the dashed horizontal in this row indicates a factual improvement. The bottom right curve indicates a correction effect between −.7 and 0, along the partisan spectrum.

Note: *** p < .001, ** p < .01, * p <.05

prohibited the United States from building new coal plants, while permitting China and India to do so. As subjects who saw (or heard) a correction were told, this was incorrect. The Paris Accords only set overall emissions targets, containing no binding mandates. We did not have a neutral source like NASA to point to; those exposed to the correction were told that Trump was wrong, and that the Paris Accord only set nonbinding targets (Kessler and Lee 2017). Afterward, all subjects had to tell us whether they agreed that "The Paris Climate Agreement required the U.S. to close coal power plants, while allowing China and India to build coal power plants," as measured on a five-point scale. (The text of the misstatements and corrections is in the online Appendix. Additional details are in Porter, Wood, and Bahador 2019.[20])

Figure 4.2 displays correction effects on beliefs about the Paris Climate Accord, conditioning on partisanship, with results displayed for both modes, and the combination of both. Turkers appear to be more affected by the correction than their telephone counterparts. When pooling across modes – thereby including more older, white, Republican respondents – we observe a positive, significant correction effect. The average correction effect was .3, in the direction of greater accuracy, on our five-point scale.

Did subjects exposed to a correction adopt different policy views? In both climate change experiments, we asked subjects how aggressive they believe environmental regulations should be. We asked: "Some people think we need tougher government regulations on business to protect the environment. Others think that the current regulations are already too burdensome. Which of the following statements comes closest to your view?" Subjects could then choose from "We need tougher regulations to protect the environment" or "Regulations are already too much of a burden." For both studies, across modes, there was no effect of seeing a correction on policy attitudes.

The State of the Union Study

As Trump's presidency wore on, two intertwined possibilities emerged. The first would be that given his penchant for mistruths and his reflexive denigration of the media, those who shared his political beliefs would come to view the rejection of corrective information as part of their own political identities. With time and repetition, they may very well have learned, from Trump himself, that corrections amount to no more than attacks on the president. Their capacity to distinguish fact from fiction would therefore be diminished. They would be

---

[20] Specifically, we asked: "Do you agree or disagree with the following statement: The Paris Climate Agreement required the U.S. to close coal power plants, while allowing China and India to build new coal power plants." As earlier, the one-to-five response scale ranged from "Strongly disagree" to "Strongly agree."

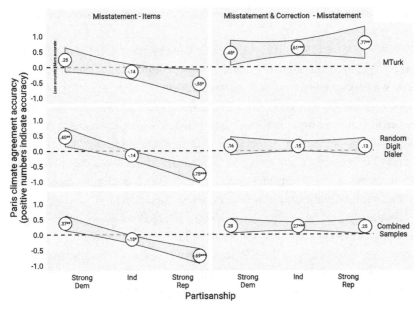

Figure 4.2 Correction effects and their 95 percent confidence intervals on the Paris Climate Accord, by partisanship. Both columns report *differences* in fitted values drawn from models that interact respondents' partisanship and the experimental condition. The left column compares those who saw the misstatement with those who only read the survey item; the right column compares those who saw the misstatement with those who saw the misstatement *and* a correction. Contrasts above the dashed horizontal indicate an accuracy improvement.

heavily incentivized to counter-argue the facts, therefore undermining one of the main claims of our theoretical argument: that such basic facts are not important enough to occasion counter-arguing. Second, Trump's constant engagement with inaccurate content might lead all subjects to regard any claims related to truth and falsehood skeptically. Trump's prevalence for lying, on this concern, would gradually curtail most subjects' ability to treat factually accurate information *as if it were accurate*. They would instead view fact and fiction indistinguishably. This worry would be most acute when empirical evidence flattered Trump.

We designed two experiments to evaluate these concerns. We administered both experiments on the night of Trump's 2019 State of the Union Address. Using Mechanical Turk, five days before the address, we gathered demographic information and asked subjects if they would be able to watch television on the night of the address (without explicitly mentioning it). We

then incentivized some to watch the address and complete a survey immediately afterward.[21]

To evaluate the effects of corrections on Trump misstatements two years into
his presidency, on the night of his address we identified a misstatement of his to
test. We wanted a high-stakes misstatement that had clear implications for his
policy agenda. Using such a misstatement would represent a hard test of the first
concern: that those on Trump's side had grown inoculated to correction efforts
with time. About halfway through his speech, Trump asserted: "My administration has sent to the Congress a commonsense proposal to end the crisis on our
southern border. . . . The lawless state of our southern border is a threat to the
safety, security, and financial well-being of all Americans."

On the night of the address, we randomly assigned some subjects to see just
this misstatement, while others were randomly assigned to see the following
correction: "According to the US Border Patrol, arrests of those attempting to
cross our southern border are at, or near, 20 year lows. Compared to the late
1990s, arrests at our southern border have declined by over 75%." (Other
contemporaneous fact-checkers also pointed to this data on the night of the
address to rebut Trump's claims about immigration; see, for example Lybrand
et al. [2019].) All subjects were asked to agree with the following statement on
our standard one-to-five-point scale: "A surge in illegal crossings is causing an
unprecedented crisis on our southern border."

In the second experiment, to test the possibility that Trump's prevalence for
misinformation may have caused a broad decline in all subjects' capacity to
separate fact from fiction, we looked for claims of his that might *sound* false but
actually reflected existing evidence. We chose the following Trump statement:
"The fact is, we are just getting started. Wages are rising at the fastest pace in
decades, and growing for blue-collar workers, who I promise to fight for. They
are growing faster than anyone else." If Trump's habitual lying were degrading
the public's underlying relationship to factual accuracy, then *affirming* the
accuracy of a true Trump claim would have no detectable effect on people's
beliefs about the claim. Indeed, it might even cause his political opponents to
backfire.

Conversely, if the public's penchant for truth had survived Trump, then
affirming one of his claims should make beliefs about the claim more accurate.
In this experiment, after assigning all subjects to see the aforementioned Trump
claim about wages, we assigned subjects to see this affirmation: "According to
the Labor Department, and a recent report by the Conference Board, this is true:

---

[21] This study was part of a larger omnibus study about presidential communication, described in
Howell, Porter, and Wood (2017).

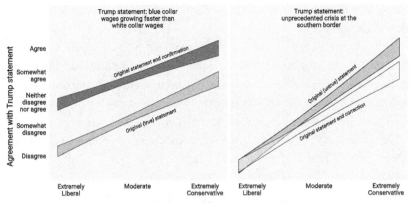

Figure 4.3 Correction and affirmation effects during the 2019 State of the Union Address. In each facet, the middle gray ribbon shows the relationship between ideology and agreement with two Trump statements made during the address: one true, concerning the relative change in blue- and white-collar wages (in the left facet), and one false, concerning the unprecedented immigration crisis at the southern border (in the right facet). Respondents in the left facet who also saw an *affirmation* that Trump's statement about white-collar wages was true are depicted in the darkest ribbon. People on the right facet who also saw a *correction* are depicted in the white ribbon. Higher values indicate agreement with Trump's statement.

blue collar wages are rising faster than white collar wages." Then, all subjects had to agree or disagree with this statement, on the same five-point scale as earlier: "Blue collar wages are currently growing faster than white collar wages."

Results appear in Figure 4.3. The right side displays effects for the misinformation experiment. The results are stark. On the same night as Trump's State of the Union Address, shortly after Trump's immigration policy preferences had provoked the longest government shutdown in history, *conservatives* who saw a correction to his misleading claim about immigration became more accurate. Rather than corroborating the first concern, that Trump's repeated misinformation would have gradually quelled his supporters' ability to be made more accurate, our evidence undermines it altogether.

The left panel of Figure 4.3 displays effects for the affirmation experiment. For every ideological group, being exposed to factually affirming evidence increased accuracy. Importantly for our substantive concern, liberals responded to the factually accurate information by becoming more accurate. If they had responded by backfiring or displaying ambivalence, then one might wonder if

Trump had taken a toll on people's ability to separate fact from fiction. This didn't happen.

Well into the Trump presidency, when provided with a correction about an issue central to his political identity, conservatives became more accurate; when an accomplishment of his was confirmed with empirical evidence, liberals became more accurate, too. Once again, this time taking a starkly different approach, we find that accuracy can be improved with ease. In sum, the evidence does not support two possible fears about the Trump presidency's effects on the public's relationship with factual accuracy.

The Trump Effect, Isolated

When provided a correction, even Trump's supporters are not swayed by his falsehoods. The results of our experiments, however, have evidently not reached Trump himself; as president, he has continued to make demonstrably false claims. In October 2018, before the midterm elections, he authored an editorial in *USA Today* in which he unleashed a bevy of false statements. *USA Today* took the unusual step of publishing a lengthy fact-check of its own article.

Does Trump have an unusual ability to sow belief in falsehoods? The publication of Trump's op-ed afforded us several opportunities for experimentation. We varied the author's identity, substituting Trump for another Republican. In addition, since Trump's election, a fact-checking apparatus had diligently fact-checked his many misstatements. Using this op-ed, we wished to test the effectiveness of the fact-checks that media organizations were regularly using on the president.

Titled "Democrats 'Medicare for All' plan will demolish promises to seniors," Trump's op-ed advanced two falsehoods. The first was that Democrats planned to enact a "Medicare for All" policy that would reduce the amount spent on programs for the elderly. The second was that the Democrats' plans represented the party's leftward drift toward South American–style socialism.

The Washington Post's Glenn Kessler wrote a lengthy fact-check of the op-ed. "Almost every sentence ... contained a misleading statement or a falsehood," Kessler began. As he explained, Sanders's plan would mandate *increased* government benefits for seniors, and the invocation of Venezuela was simply absurd. "We are unaware of any Democratic leader who has pointed to Venezuela as an economic model," wrote Kessler.

Participants were randomly assigned to see either Trump's op-ed alone or Trump's op-ed paired with Kessler's fact-check. To isolate the effects of Trump on misinformation and corrections, we assigned other subjects to see the same editorial, but with authorship attributed to Republican Senate leader Mitch McConnell. Those who saw the McConnell version of the article also saw a version of the fact-checking article, modified to read as if it were correcting McConnell, not Trump. Some subjects were assigned to control, seeing no article and no correction.

We slightly modified the Trump and McConnell articles so that the only differences between them was the name of the author. These changes mean that differences in correction effects are attributable *only* to the different authors. The op-eds and corrections can be found in the online Appendix.

We asked all subjects to agree with the following statements on a one-to-five agree-disagree scale:

- The Democratic Party wants to slash budgets for Medicare and Social Security
- The Democratic Party views Venezuela as a model for America's economy

The first statement was unambiguously false. Medicare for All, were it to be implemented, would not *slash* budgets. The second statement, despite Kessler's wry observation that no Democrats *actually* advocate for modeling America's economy on Venezuela's, was closer to typical embellished attacks on the counter-party. We also asked subjects to state their approval of McConnell and Trump along a one-to-five scale.

The average participant, even the average Republican, responded to corrections by becoming more accurate. However, effects were larger for McConnell's op-ed than for Trump's. That is, being assigned to a correction about a McConnell misstatement prompted larger gains in accuracy than being assigned to a correction about Trump – though the only difference between the articles and the fact-checks was supposed authorship.

Figures 4.4 and 4.5 display results for both questions. We observed larger accuracy increases regarding Medicare than regarding the Venezuela comparison. Extreme conservatives who read the McConnell story and were exposed to the Medicare correction evinced the largest movement toward accuracy of any ideological group. However, we observed no increases for conservatives for the same article, when virtually all that differed was the author's name. When we show the difference in correction effects between McConnell and Trump on the Medicare question, for conservatives, the difference between the two authors was significant. A similar pattern is evident in response to the Venezuela question. To put this in perspective, among conservatives responding to the Medicare question, the accuracy increase following McConnell was more than *thirteen* times larger than it was on Trump. It was about twice as large on the Venezuela question (though not significantly so).

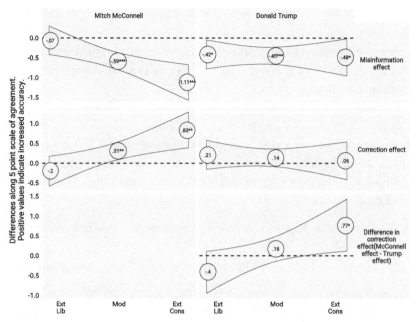

Figure 4.4 Correction effects, and their 95 percent confidence intervals, for McConnell and Trump's misstatements on Democrats and Medicare. In the left facet, respondents were told that McConnell made the misstatement; in the right facet, it was Trump. The second row shows the effect of a correction on accuracy; larger values indicate better accuracy. The third row indicates the difference in effects between McConnell and Trump. Larger values in the third row indicate better responsiveness to McConnell than to Trump.

Figure 4.6 details how corrections targeting McConnell and Trump differentially affected the share of accurate respondents. For both questions, we look at how subjects' ideological views relate to accuracy gains owed to corrections. We identify subjects as "accurate" if they somewhat or strongly disagreed with the false proposition, and "inaccurate" if they somewhat or strongly agreed with it. When authorship of the misinformation was attributed to McConnell, only 18 percent of conservatives who did not see a correction accurately responded that the Democrats were against Social Security cuts. Only 19 percent of conservatives not shown a correction accurately rejected the statement that Democrats favored Venezuelan socialism. However, among conservatives shown a correction to those misstatements when they were attributed to McConnell, 38 percent and 33 percent expressed accurate views.

In contrast, corrections to Trump *did not* meaningfully increase the share of conservatives who expressed accurate views, compared to non-corrected

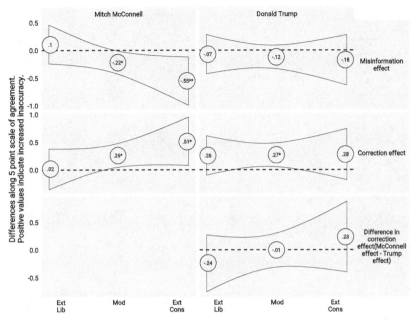

Figure 4.5 Correction effects, and their 95 percent confidence intervals, for McConnell's and Trump's misstatements on Democrats and Venezuela. In the left facet, respondents were told that McConnell made the misstatement; in the right facet, it was Trump. The second row shows the effect of a correction on accuracy; larger values indicate better accuracy. The third row indicates the difference in effects between McConnell and Trump. Larger values in the third row indicate better responsiveness to McConnell than to Trump.

conservatives who viewed the misstatements attributed to McConnell. By this metric, corrections *reduced* the share of accurate conservatives, though not significantly so. This suggests that conservatives are protective of their co-partisan president. No similar patterns exist for moderates and liberals. Corrections to Trump prompted larger increases in the share of accurate moderates than did corrections to McConnell. Across all subjects, corrections to the Venezuelan misstatement prompted larger gains in the share of accurate respondents when attributed to McConnell, while corrections to the socialism misstatement did the opposite.

As expected, we did not observe corrections having any effects on approval toward either politician. Even when a correction increases accuracy, attitudes toward politicians are more stable. Approval of both politicians remained constant even among those who only saw the misstatement, without a correction. This implied that while Trump's misstatements can – when not

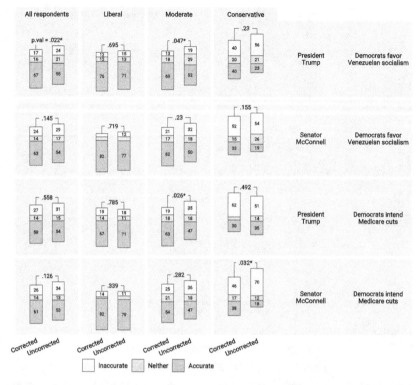

Figure 4.6 The effectiveness of correction on reducing incorrect perceptions, by ideological affiliation (in the column facets) and corrected speakers and issues (in the rows). Each facet includes the p-value associated with that facet's chi^2 test. P-values significant at the .05 level annotated.

Note:　*** p < .001, ** p < .01, * p < .05

paired with a correction – misinform the citizenry, he reaps no obvious political benefits from them. We designed the next experiment to test this implication.

A Political Price to Pay?

We have shown that when followed by a correction, President Trump's misinformation can be rebutted. Does he pay a political price, however, for these corrections? While the RNC study showed that his approval remained constant despite exposure to one correction that was administered during the presidential campaign. Moreover, we only tested the effects of single corrections in that study. Since then, not only has Trump assumed the White House, but he has also continued to unleash a barrage of misstatements – which, in turn, have been greeted by an energetic fact-checking industry. When he misleads and is fact-checked, does he suffer political consequences among those who see a fact-check? Conversely, when he misleads *and is not fact-checked*, does he gain some advantage?

To find out, we tested the effects of multiple fact-checks targeting Trump and multiple misstatements by Trump not followed by a fact-check on presidential approval. Subjects were assigned to see one to three misstatements made by Trump, one to three corrections of those misstatements, or to a pure control. Subjects were then asked Gallup's presidential approval question: "Do you approve or disapprove of the way Donald Trump is handling his job as president?" Subjects could answer "Approve," "Disapprove," or "No Opinion." We focused on approval because it proxies well for perceptions of presidential power and leverage (e.g., Ponder 2017). Trump himself tweets frequently about his approval ratings, boasting when he believes them to be high. Whether or not his ratings are improved due to his misstatements – or whether they are hurt by the corrections that follow – is an open question.

In selecting Trump misstatements to use here, we looked for misstatements that he plausibly could have delivered with the aim of improving people's attitudes toward him. For one such misstatement, we reused the *USA Today* op-ed we tested in the previous study. For another misstatement, we used a sentence he uttered during his 2019 State of the Union. "We have unleashed a revolution in American energy – the United States is now the No. 1 producer of oil and natural gas in the world," he said then. Finally, we turned to a misstatement he made on Twitter. "More people working in U.S.A. today than at any other time in our HISTORY!" he wrote.

As usual, we carefully mimicked the fact-checks that had been made of these exact statements. As FactCheck.org pointed out after Trump's aforementioned tweet, employment totals that do not take into account population are not particularly meaningful.[22] Our correction read as follows: "The statistic that Trump pointed to does not take into account population growth. According to the Bureau of Labor Statistics, the employment-to-population ratio, which measures the percentage of population that is employed, actually peaked in the year 2000 – long before Trump became president." For the claim about oil and gas, contemporaneous fact-checks (e.g., Woodward, Yen, and Rugaber 2019) pointed out that the trend Trump was touting began under Obama. The correction we provided pointed to Obama explicitly: "When it comes to oil and gas production, Trump built on Obama's accomplishments. According to government data, the U.S. became the world's top natural gas producer in 2013, when Obama was president." To correct Trump's *USA Today* op-ed, we reused Kessler's fact-check. In sum, the corrections subjects saw were provocative –

---

[22] See the FactCheck.org correction here: https://bit.ly/2H94jHv.

giving credit to Obama by name, for example – and ranged from single sentences to multiple paragraphs.

The experiment was administered over Mechanical Turk in February 2019. After answering demographic questions, subjects were assigned to see one to three misstatements, one to three misstatements and corrections, or neither. Corrections and misstatements were always presented in random order.

Only in the conditions in which subjects were exposed to the maximal number of misstatements or corrections did we observe effects on approval. In all other conditions, we were unable to detect any effects. Exposure to three misstatements by Trump boosted the probability that a voter would approve of him by .07. Conversely, exposure to three corrections of those misstatements decreased that probability by .07. It's worth underlining, however, that these effects are only weakly significant. (A full regression table appears in the online Appendix.) Note that our results are likely not a function of statistical power; indeed, we were as well powered for this experiment as we were for our previous experiments. If corrections and misinformation matter for approval, they do so only slightly, and roughly in equal amounts.

Different misstatements and corrections might have yielded different results. More likely, however, is that citizens' views of politicians are not strongly affected by corrections. Tempered by statistical ambiguity, we can only conclude that a sizable number of misstatements can nudge Trump's approval up, while the same number can nudge them down by about the same amount. Whether Trump pays a political price for his misstatements may be up to fact-checkers.

Discussion

Is Trump different? On many matters, the answer is obviously yes. He is willing to make claims at odds with the facts more readily than his predecessors. Conservatives are not made nearly as accurate by corrections of his misstatements as they are of misstatements by Mitch McConnell, holding the misstatement constant. However, as we have shown repeatedly, *on average*, Americans exposed to a correction after a Trump misstatement are made more accurate.

Why do conservatives respond differently to corrections attributed to him than to McConnell? We can think of several reasons. The first presumes that Trump himself is *not* unique. Presidents inspire unique loyalty among co-partisans (e.g., Lenz 2012). That having been said, we did not observe a similar defensiveness among Democrats about Obama and factual corrections at the end of his administration. One way of reconciling this disparity is considering that near the end of an administration, partisans may become less reluctant to correct their co-partisan president than they are at the beginning of a co-partisan administration. If so, Republicans should be more affected by corrections to Trump as his presidency wears on. This is a testable proposition that we plan to keep an eye on.

The second possibility relates to the idea that, indeed, Trump is different – that he has an unusual ability to sow misinformation, and that his supporters appreciate it when he does (Halh, Kim, and Sivan 2018). When a Trump misstatement is *not* followed up with a correction, Trump can convince people of falsehoods. In the Trump/McConnell experiment, control subjects only exposed to Trump's misstatement, and not a correction, agreed more with the inaccurate position. Such effects are visible in the top panels of Figures 4.4 and 4.5. We also observed this in other experiments of ours, when Trump was not the one advancing the misstatement. The capacity of false statements to reduce accuracy should not be surprising: without contrary information, subjects in a vacuum may well come to agree with a misstatement. But when a Trump misstatement is paired with a correction, no average subject, *including the average Republican and average conservative*, has become more inaccurate. This has been the case in every experiment we've conducted.

Perhaps most importantly, as we show in the final experiment, any gains Trump makes by misleading people are matched in size by the losses he suffers when he is corrected. While the appeal of the lying demagogue is real, through continued correction that appeal can be blunted. Either way, however, one-off instances of corrections and misstatements do not affect approval ratings. As the argument we lay out in the Section 1 makes clear, political attitudes and partisan preferences are at most distantly related to empirical evidence. The distance between the two is precisely why subjects can be made more factually accurate by corrections without changing their related attitudes.

5 Conclusion

Americans are more responsive to factual information than bleak portrayals lead one to expect. This isn't to say that Americans form their political attitudes based on the available evidence. Yet during the 2016 presidential election and well into the Trump administration, on an enormous variety of issues, corrections increased accuracy, if only for a short amount of time. Greater accuracy, however, did not mostly come with changed policy attitudes. While the volume of his misinformation can improve views toward Trump, such views can also be degraded by an equal number of corrections.

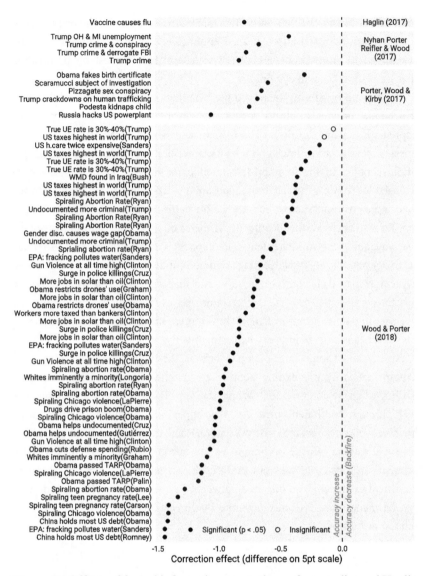

Figure 5.1 Effects of factual information across three of our studies and Haglin (2017).

To understand the breadth and depth of the issues on which accuracy can be improved, consider Figure 5.1, which showcases the average correction effect across a range of items. On the far left, we include results from Haglin's (2017) study on corrections. At no point in any of our studies or in Haglin's did average subjects "backfire," or otherwise increase their belief in an erroneous position. Instead, on average, people responded to corrections by increasing their level of agreement with the accurate position. As we've plotted the effects in order of their size, on the far right in Figure 5.1 appear two items on which we failed to observe significant accuracy increases – that is, two items on which people who saw the correction were not meaningfully more accurate from those who did not. But again, we never observed backfire. Importantly, these effects are of meaningful size. Across all our experiments, we average an effect of −.81 along a five-point scale (where a negative value indicates less agreement with the false position).

To get a sense of the magnitude, we can compare it to the absolute ideological differences in opinion among uncorrected subjects. Compared to the maximum ideological difference in factual beliefs – comparing, in other words, the difference in factual beliefs between extreme liberals and extreme conservatives not exposed to a correction – the average effect is around the fortieth percentile of this ideological difference.[23] In other words, a *single* correction is about as influential on factual beliefs as moving halfway along the ideological divide. Backfire is a *very* low bar for citizen competence – and on average, citizens clear this bar.

After exposure to a correction, how many of our subjects expressed accurate views? The bottom right of Table 5.1 offers answers. Across all our studies, we find that 59.9 percent of all subjects who had seen a correction subsequently expressed accurate beliefs. Among those who had not seen a correction, only 31.9 percent expressed accurate beliefs. Exposure to a correction increased the share of accurate responses by 28 percentage points. Or as the bottom right-hand cells show, 46.6 percent of respondents who had not seen a correction were inaccurate, but only 24.7 percent of subjects who had seen a correction were inaccurate. In sum, without a correction, nearly half of responses given to our often-demanding questions were inaccurate. With a correction, fewer than a quarter were.

To construct Table 5.1, we aggregated responses from all studies in which we randomly exposed some subjects to a correction and measured agreement with the inaccurate positions. (This accounts for all studies in this Element except the approval study from Section 4.) Responses from subjects who slightly or strongly disagreed with the inaccurate position were regarded as being accurate, and vice versa.[24] The table also displays how the ideology of the respondent and the ideology of the speaker related to accuracy increases. This relationship matters. A full 64 percent of conservatives exposed to a correction of a liberal speaker were subsequently accurate, while 39.7 percent of conservatives exposed to a correction of

---

[23] This figure is calculated by taking the absolute value of the difference in factual beliefs between strong conservatives and strong liberals in control, for all issues in all studies.

[24] For studies in which we asked people to agree with the accurate position, we used the reverse coding.

Table 5.1 Overall correction effects, by respondent ideology and speaker ideology. Cell entries underneath the column labels are row percentages, reporting accuracy of respondents' factual attitudes. They are next to a column that reports sample sizes. Italicized text reports the *difference* in these row percentages between the corrected and uncorrected respondents. Finally, in the bottom right of the table, we report the factual accuracy of respondents, averaging over their ideologies and the ideologies of the corrected respondents.

		Liberal Speakers				Conservative Speakers				All Speakers			
		Accurate	Neither	Inaccurate	N	Accurate	Neither	Inaccurate	N	Accurate	Neither	Inaccurate	N
Liberals	Correction	52.7	16.3	30.9	3,713	74.8	11.5	13.7	6,123	65.7	13.5	20.8	9,836
	No Correction	21.0	17.8	61.2	3,635	50.0	21.6	28.4	6,213	38.0	20.0	42.0	9,848
	Difference	*31.7*	*−1.5*	*−30.3*		*24.8*	*−10.1*	*−14.7*		*27.7*	*−6.5*	*−21.2*	
Moderates	Correction	57.2	16.7	26.1	4,612	60.4	17.1	22.5	6,933	59.0	17.0	24.1	11,545
	No Correction	26.2	21.4	52.4	4,549	31.6	25.5	42.9	6,971	29.2	23.7	47.0	11,520
	Difference	*31.0*	*−4.7*	*−26.3*		*28.8*	*−8.4*	*−20.4*		*29.8*	*−6.7*	*−22.9*	
Conservatives	Correction	64.0	12.2	23.8	1,444	39.7	17.3	43.0	2,978	48.9	15.4	35.7	4,422
	No Correction	35.9	17.1	47.0	1,422	19.5	19.3	61.2	3,361	25.3	18.5	56.2	4,783
	Difference	*28.1*	*−4.9*	*−23.2*		*20.2*	*−2.0*	*−18.2*		*23.6*	*−3.1*	*−20.5*	
All Respondents	Correction	56.5	15.9	27.6	9,769	62.1	15.0	22.9	16,034	**59.9**	**15.4**	**24.7**	25,803
	No Correction	25.6	19.4	55.0	9,606	36.0	22.8	41.2	16,545	**31.9**	**21.4**	**46.6**	26,151
	Difference	*30.9*	*−3.5*	*−27.4*		*26.1*	*−7.8*	*−18.3*		***28.0***	***−6.0***	***−21.9***	

a conservative speaker were subsequently accurate. Yet even among conservatives who saw a correction to a conservative speaker, corrections increased the share of accurate responses by 20.2 percentage points. When we look at how both liberals and conservatives responded to all misstatements, we see corrections prompting similar declines in the share of inaccurate responses – 21.2 and 20.5 percentage points, respectively.

Across political views, and across an enormous range of issues, the evidence is clear: When it comes to accuracy, corrections work. This conclusion corroborates our theoretical argument. Corrections, whether applied to political or nonpolitical misinformation, have little trouble improving accuracy. Yet accuracy improvements do not often change policy attitudes. To us, this indicates that subjects can pursue accuracy *and* partisan goals at the same time. When asked an empirical question about which they have accurate information at their disposal, they respond with that information in mind, even if the information cuts against a co-partisan's claim. Their views about policy, however, appear unaffected.

But corrections do not eliminate inaccuracies. After corrections, many people still believe falsehoods. The problem appears more acute with conservatives; in our data, 35.7 percent of conservatives were still inaccurate after seeing a correction, compared to only 20.8 percent of liberals. In part, this discrepancy can be attributed to differing baseline levels of accurate knowledge. While 38 percent of liberals were accurate without a correction, only 25.3 percent of conservatives were. The different baselines explain why the accuracy increases and inaccuracy decreases were roughly similar for both groups. Fact-checking efforts must more aggressively target conservative citizens – and they should do so without fear of backfire.

In this landscape, do politicians have incentives to be truthful? The implications of our evidence on this are mixed. When not followed by a correction, misinformation can increase inaccuracy. Enough misinformation can even boost the approval of the politician disseminating the misinformation. At the same time, corrections disabuse people of misinformation, and an equivalent number of corrections can reduce the approval of that same politician. If politicians who spread misinformation are confident that they can stay one step ahead of the fact-checkers, then, indeed, they have an incentive to lie. Whether politicians have sufficient incentives to be truthful will ultimately depend on fact-checkers keeping up with the pace of misinformation and convincing consumers of misinformation to read their fact-checks.

This brings to mind one of the central limitations of our results. Our conclusion hinges on presenting corrections. Individuals who encounter a misleading statement or a fake story without subsequently encountering a correction may very well come to hold inaccurate beliefs. Evidence suggests that consumers of fake news virtually never consume corrections of those fake stories on their own (Nyhan, Reifler, and Guess 2017). Our evidence shows that among those who consume fact-checks, accuracy gains are short lived. For the sake of an informed public, media companies should fact-check aggressively.

Observational evidence further indicates that the public is surprisingly factually accurate. In three of the more infamous examples of supposed ignorance, the public has gradually become more accurate. Take climate change. In Figure 5.2, we harness Pew data to show attitudes about the source of climate change. Today, more than twice as many people agree with the scientifically sound proposition that humans are responsible for climate change. Indeed, more than 50 percent of Americans accept the scientific consensus on this issue, with "only a few" denying climate change altogether (Hamilton et al. 2015). Against a well-funded industry campaign to convince them otherwise (e.g., Oreskes and Conway 2010), the majority of Americans have come to accept settled science.

The public has also had to confront a well-funded effort to downplay or deny the link between cigarettes and cancer (Brandt 2012; Heath 2016). Yet as Figure 5.3 illustrates with Gallup data, the public's commitment to science is stark. Overwhelmingly, in the face of a sophisticated effort to convince them otherwise, Americans acknowledge the science here. Cigarettes cause cancer, and the vast majority know it. Or consider evolution. As Figure 5.4 shows, based on Gallup data, the number of Americans who report believing in evolution has nearly doubled this century. Of course, many people still profess a version of creationism or other forms of divine involvement. Yet those numbers are on the decline.

Naturally, there are exceptions to this pattern – instances in which people have proven stubbornly resistant to accuracy. But on these well-known, contentious debates, people have incrementally become more accurate. These observational patterns echo our experiments. When presented with accurate information, people become more accurate. We offer one critical caveat: this seems to be true when the matters being tested concern basic facts, for which there is no room for dispute. Regarding more ambiguous questions, the partisan screen continues to play a large, possibly increasing role. Jones (2019), for example, shows that retrospective evaluations of the economy and foreign policy have grown more polarized along partisan lines. Such evaluations, however, are qualitatively distinct from the basic factual matters we test here.

Why do some observers insist that the public is spectacularly resistant to accurate information? We can think of three possible reasons. One explanation recalls that, in fact, none of these concerns is new. While Donald Trump's

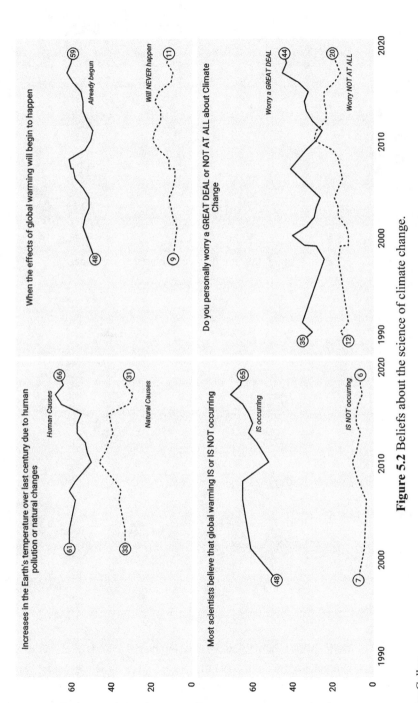

Figure 5.2 Beliefs about the science of climate change.

Source: Gallup.

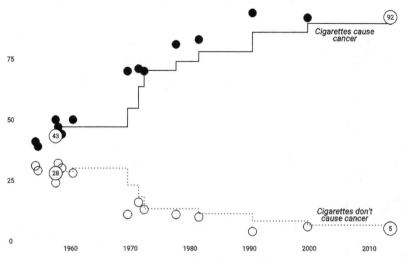

Figure 5.3 Beliefs about the link between cigarettes and cancer.
Source: Gallup.

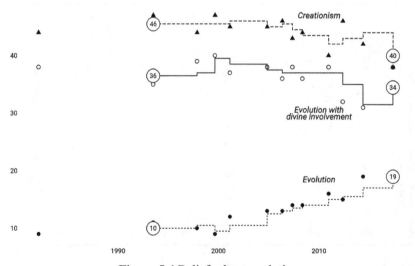

Figure 5.4 Beliefs about evolution.
Source: Gallup.

election may have amplified them, they are part and parcel of a set of anxieties about citizens' competence for democracy that predates Trump. These anxieties can be traced back to ancient Greece. In *The Republic*, Socrates argues that unless "political power and philosophic intelligence converge," with only the most intelligent people making political decisions, civilization will be in constant peril. The learned should rule; but "the multitude" is incapable of learning (Sterling and Scott 1985). Democracy's insistence on including the multitude in political decision making may lead one to worry: What if the multitude is not capable of responsibly making the kinds of decisions necessary in democracy? Those who advance accounts of citizens being unable to accept political facts are effectively answering this question in the negative. Some of the interest in portraying citizens as factually maladaptive may be normatively motivated. It is little wonder that the evidence on citizens' difficulties with facts is sometimes marshaled to explicitly argue against democracy (e.g., Brennan 2016).

Another explanation might be called "the crazy uncle phenomenon." We all have a crazy uncle, or know someone who qualifies as such: a person who refuses to accept facts *qua* facts, whose political views are extreme, and who regards fringe conspiracy theories as the historical record. These people surely exist. They are vividly memorable. However, crazy uncles are, numerically, few and far between. Upon reflection, this makes sense. If most families have *a* crazy uncle, that also means, by definition, that most members of most families are *not* crazy uncles. Most people's political views are, instead, sane, predictable, and maybe even a little dull.

But the crazy uncles of our lives are memorable – and their memorableness matters. When making estimates of the frequency of certain types or classes, people tend to rely on easily retrievable, provocative examples. In their explanation of the availability heuristic, Kahneman and Tversky describe a (hypothetical) clinician asked to assess a depressive patient. If one of the clinician's other patients has recently attempted suicide, then the clinician may overestimate the probability that this new patient will also attempt suicide (Kahneman and Tversky 1973, pp. 228–29).

It is a morbid but telling example. By analogy, when people think about Americans' relationship to political facts, they may think of the family member or friend (or Facebook friend) who makes wild, fact-free claims and then extrapolate this person onto the population as a whole. Consequently, their impression of the public will be skewed, away from the perspective of the less memorable individuals whom they encounter most often, and toward those who they encounter less but whose views stand out. Ultimately, they dramatically overestimate the prevalence of crazy uncles, thereby neglecting their certifiably non-crazy family members, not to mention vast numbers of Americans.

A third possible explanation focuses on political elites. Perhaps elites are comparatively more likely to cling to misstatements than the mass public. Such a finding would make some theoretical sense; as Zaller (1992) argues, people with richer ideological attachments are less susceptible to new information that comes their way. It's not as though political elites can't be persuaded to change their minds (e.g., Coppock, Ekins, and Kirby 2018) Rather, it's that elites may be systematically more likely to reject corrections than the average non-elite. This disparity may be in part responsible for the sense of crisis described in the Section 1. The crisis, as it were, relates to the general impression that political officeholders have trouble discerning fact from fiction. The current president does little to dispel this notion; if Donald Trump had been enrolled as a respondent in our experiments, it would not be so surprising if he had backfired.

In describing public opinion toward misinformation in general, however – separate from Trump as an individual – the picture is more mundane. People often are made more accurate by facts, even if facts challenge their political commitments. But they attach no special importance to facts. Ultimately, we suspect that some of the concern over supposed factual maladaptivity is standing in for an underlying concern about political attitudes. *If only people knew the facts about politics, their attitudes would change.* So the thinking goes. This view is likely overstated. Political attitudes, particularly when they are enmeshed in partisanship and the presidency, have at best a distant relationship to facts. Yet this doesn't mean people are, as a matter of reflex, factually maladaptive. Instead, when shown a fact, they seem to shrug and accept it. This is not the most colorful conclusion. But it seems to be the one that comes closest to matching the facts.

References

Abramowitz, A. (2010). *The Disappearing Center*. New Haven: Yale University Press.

Achen, C. and L. Bartels. (2016). *Democracy for Realists: Why Elections Do Not Produce Responsive Government*. Princeton, NJ: Princeton University Press.

Allcott, H. and M. Gentzkow. (2017). "Social Media and Fake News in the 2016 Election." *Journal of Economic Perspectives*. 31 (2): 211–35.

The American National Election Studies. (2018). *The ANES Guide to Public Opinion and Electoral Behavior* (www.electionstudies.org).

Ansolabehere, S. and D. M. Konisky. (2014). *Cheap and Clean: How Americans Think about Energy in the Age of Global Warming*. Cambridge, MA: MIT Press.

Arendt, H. (1971). *Crises of the Republic*. Orlando: Harcourt Brace and Company.

Bartels, L. (2002). "Beyond the Running Tally: Partisan Bias in Political Perception." *Political Behavior*. 24 (2): 117–50.

Benegal, S. D. and L. A. Scruggs. (2018). "Correcting Misinformation About Climate Change: The Impact of Partisanship in an Experimental Setting." *Climactic Change*. 148: 61–80.

Berelson, B. R., P. Lazarsfield, and W. N. McPhee. (1954). *Voting: A Study of Opinion Formation in a Presidential Campaign*. Chicago: University of Chicago Press.

Berinsky, A. J. (2017). "Rumors and Health Care Reform: Experiments in Political Misinformation." *British Journal of Political Science*. 47 (2): 241–62.

   G. A. Huber, and G. S. Lenz. (2012). "Evaluating Online Labor Markets for Experimental Research: Amazon.com's Mechanical Turk." *Political Analysis*. 20: 351–68.

Boxell, L., M. Gentzkow and J. M. Shapiro. (2018). "A Note on Internet Use and the 2016 U.S. Presidential Election Outcome." *PLoS ONE*. 13 (7): e0199571. https://doi.org/10.1371/journal. pone.0199571

Brandt, A. M. (2012). "Inventing Conflicts of Interest: A History of Tobacco Industry Tactics." *American Journal of Public Health*. 102 (1): 63–71.

Brennan, J. (2016). *Against Democracy*. Princeton, NJ: Princeton University Press.

Bullock, J. G. (2009). "Partisan Bias and the Bayesian Ideal in the Study of Public Opinion." *Journal of Politics*. 71 (July): 1109–24.

A. S. Gerber, S. J. Hill, and G. A. Huber. (2015). "Partisan Bias in Factual Beliefs about Politics." *Quarterly Journal of Political Science.* 10: 519–78.

Burns, E. (2006.) *Infamous Scribblers: The Founding Fathers and the Rowdy Beginnings of American Journalism.* New York: Public Affairs.

Campbell, A., P. E. Converse, W. E. Miller, and D. E. Stokes. (1960). *The American Voter.* Chicago: University of Chicago Press.

Carpini, M. X. D. and S. Keeter. (1996). *What Americans Know About Politics and Why It Matters.* New Haven: Yale University Press.

Chan, M. P. S., C. R. Jones, K. H. Jamieson, and D. Albarracín. (2017). "Debunking: A Meta-Analysis of the Psychological Efficacy of Messages Countering Misinformation." *Psychological Science.* 28 (11): 1531–46.

Chen, X., P. Tsaparas, J. Lijffijt, and T. D. Bie. 2019. "Opinion Dynamics with Backfire Effect and Biased Assimilation." Accessed via https://arxiv.org/pdf/1903.11535.pdf

Chong, D. and J. N. Druckman. (2007). "Framing Theory." *Annual Review of Political Science.* 10: 103–26.

Cochran, W. G., and G. M. Cox. (1957). *Experimental Designs.* New York: John Wiley & Sons, Ltd.

Cordrea-Rado, A. (March 21, 2018). "Wolfgang Tillmans Explores the Role of Art in a Post-Truth World." *New York Times.*

Coppock, A. (2018). "Generalizing from Survey Experiments Conducted on Mechanical Turk: A Replication Approach." *Political Science Research and Methods.* 1–16. doi:10.1017/psrm.2018.10

E. Ekins, and D. Kirby. (2018). "The Long-lasting Effects of Newspaper Op-Eds on Public Opinion." *Quarterly Journal of Political Science.* 13 (1): 59–87.

Davison, W. P. (1983). "The Third-Person Effect in Communication." *Public Opinion Quarterly.* 47 (1): 1–15.

Downs, A. (1957). *An Economic Theory of Democracy.* New York: Harper and Row.

Druckman, J. N. (2012). "The Politics of Motivation." *Critical Review: A Journal of Politics and Society.* 24 (2): 199–216.

Ecker, K. H. U., S. Lewandowsky, and D. T. W. Wang. (2010). "Explicit Warnings Reduce But Do Not Eliminate the Continued Influence of Misinformation." *Memory and Cognition.* 38 (8): 1087–100.

Engelhardt, A. M. and S. M. Utych. (2018). "Grand Old Tailgate Party: Partisan Discrimination in Apolitical Settings." *Political Behavior.* https://doi.org/10.1007/s11109-018-09519-4

Evans, J. B. T. 2008. "Dual-Processing Accounts of Reasoning, Judgment, and Social Cognition." *Annual Review of Psychology*. 59: 255–78.

Festinger, L. (1957). *A Theory of Cognitive Dissonance*. Evanston, IL: Row, Peterson and Company.

(1950). "Informal Social Communication." *Psychological Review*. 57: 271–82.

Gaines, B. J., J. H. Kuklinski, P. J. Quirk, B. Peyton, and J. Verkuilen. (2007). "Same Facts, Different Interpretations: Partisan Motivation and Opinion On Iraq." *Journal of Politics*. 69 (4): 957–74.

Gerber, A. S. and D. P. Green. (2012). *Field Experiments: Design, Analysis and Interpretation*. New York: W. W. Norton and Company.

Glasser, S. (2016, December 2). "Covering Politics in a 'Post-Truth' America." The Brookings Institute. Accessed via www.brookings.edu/essay/cover ing-politics-in-a-post-truth-america/

Graves, L. (2016). *Deciding What's True: The Rise of Political Fact-Checking in American Journalism*. New York: Columbia University Press.

Green, D. P., B. Palmquist, and E. Schickler. (2002). *Partisan Hearts and Minds: Political Parties and the Social Identities of Voters*. New Haven, CT: Yale University Press.

Greenberg, J. (2018). "Donald Trump Gets Polar Ice Trend Backwards." *Politifact*. Accessed via www.politifact.com/truth-o-meter/statements/ 2018/jan/29/donald-trump/ trump-gets-polar-ice-trend-backwards/

Gross, K., E. Porter, and T. J. Wood. (2019). "Identifying Media Effects Through Low-Cost, Multi-Wave Field Experiments." *Political Communication*. 36 (2): 272–87.

Guess, A., J. Tucker, and J. Nagler. (2018). "Less Than You Think: Prevalence and Predictors of Fake News Dissemination on Facebook." *Science Advances*. 5 (1).

Guess, A. J. and A. Coppock. (n.d.). "Does Counterattitudinal Information Cause Backlash? Results from Three Large Survey Experiments." *British Journal of Political Science*.

B. Nyhan, and J. Reifler. (2018). "Selective Exposure to Misinformation: Evidence from the Consumption of Fake News During the 2016 U.S. Presidential Campaign." Accessed via www.dartmouth.edu/~nyhan/fake-news-2016.pdf

and A. Coppock, (Forthcoming). "Does Counter-Attitudinal Information Cause Backlash? Results from Three Large Survey Experiments." *British Journal of Politcal Science*. Accessed via https: //webspace .princeton.edu/users/aguess/GC_Backlash_Final.pdf

Haglin, K. (2017). "The Limitations of the Backfire Effect." *Research and Politics*. Accessed via https: //doi.org/10.1177/2053168017716547

Hahl, O., M. Kim, and E. W. Zuckerman Sivan. 2018. "The Authentic Appeal of the Lying Demagogue: Proclaiming the Deeper Truth about Political Illegitimacy." *American Sociological Review*. 83 (1): 1–33.

Hamilton, L. C. J. J. Hartter, J. Lemke-Stampone, M. Moore, and T. G. Safford. (2015). "Tracking Public Beliefs About Anthropogenic Climate Change." *PLOS ONE*. Accessed via https://doi.org/10. 1371/journal.pone.0138208

Heath, D. (2016). "Contesting the Science of Smoking." *The Atlantic*. Accessed via www.theatlantic.com/politics/archive/2016/05/low-tar-cigarettes/481116/

Hill, S. J. (2017). "Learning Together Slowly: Bayesian Learning About Political Facts." *Journal of Politics*. 79 (4): 1403–18.

Howell, W .G., E. Porter, and T. J. Wood. (2017). "Making a President: Performance, Public Opinion and the (Temporary) Transmutation of Donald J. Trump." Available at SSRN: https://papers.ssrn.com/sol3/papers.cfm?abstract_id=3111903

Hochschild, J. and K. L. Einstein. (2015). *Do Facts Matter?: Information and Misinformation in American Politics*. Norman: University of Oklahoma Press.

Huber, G., S. Hill, and G. Lenz. 2012. "Sources of Bias in Retrospective Decision Making: Experimental Evidence on Voters' Limitations in Controlling Incumbents." *American Political Science Review*. 106 (4): 720–41.

Isaac, M. and K. Roose. (2018). "Disinformation Spreads on WhatsApp Ahead of Brazilian Election." *New York Times*. Accessed via www.nytimes.com/2018/10/19/ technology/whatsapp-brazil-presidential-election.html?smprod=nytcore-ipad& smid=nytcore-ipad-share

Iyengar, S., G. Sood, and Y. Lelkes. 2012. "Affect, Not Ideology: A Social Identity Theory on Polarization." *Public Opinion Quarterly*. 76 (3): 405–31.

Iyengar, S. and S. J. Westwood. (2015). "Fear and Loathing Across Party Lines: New Evidence on Group Polarization." *American Journal of Political Science*. 59 (3): 690—707.

Jacobson, L. (2018). "Alexandria Ocasio-Cortez Wrong on Several Counts About Unemployment." Politifact. Accessed via www.politifact.com/truth-o-meter/statements/2018/jul/18/alexandria-ocasio-cortez/alexandria-ocasio-cortez-wrong-several-counts-abou/

Jerit, J. and J. Barabas. (2012). "Partisan Perceptual Bias and the Information Environment." *The Journal of Politics*. 74 (3): 672–84.

Johnson, H. M. and C. M. Seifert. (1998). "Updating Accounts Following a Correction of Misinformation." *Journal of Experimental Psychology: Learning, Memory, and Cognition*. 24(6): 1483–94.

Jones, P. E. (2019). "Partisanship, Political Awareness, and Retrospective Evaluations, 1956–2016." *Political Behavior.* Accessed via https://doi .org/10.1007/s11109-019-09543-y

Kahan, D. and D. Braman. (2006). "Cultural Cognition and Public Policy." *Yale Law and Policy Review.* 24 (147): 147–70.

Kaplan, J., S. I. Gimbel, and S. Harris. (2016). "Neural Correlates of Maintaining One's Political Beliefs in the Face of Counterevidence." *Nature Scientific Reports.* 6.

Kessler, G. and M. Y. H. Lee. (2017). "Fact-checking President Trump's Claims on the Paris Climate Change Deal." *Washington Post.* Accessed via www .washingtonpost.com/news/fact-checker/wp/ 192017/06/01/fact-checking -preside

Kessler, G., S. Rizzo, and M. Kelly. (2018). "President Trump Has Made 3,001 False or Misleading Claims So Far." *Washington Post.* Accessed via www .washingtonpost.com/news/fact-checker/wp/2018/05/01/president-trump-has -made-3001-false-or-misleading-claims-so-far/?utm_term=.f4222c766c67

Khaldarova, I. and M. Pantti. (2016). "Fake News: The Narrative Battle Over the Ukrainian Conflict." *Journalism Practice.* 10 (7): 891–901.

Koyre, A. (1945). "The Political Function of the Modern Lie." In *Contemporary Jewish Record.* Vol. 8. New York: American Jewish Committee.

Kuklinksi, J. H., P. J. Quirk, J. Jerit, D. Schweider, and R. F. Rich. (2000). "Misinformation and the Currency of Democratic Citizenship." *Journal of Politics.* 62 (3): 790–816.

Lazer, D. M. J, M. A. Baum, Y. Benkler, A. J. Berinsky, K. M. Greenhill, F. et al. (2018). "The Science of Fake News." *Science.* 359 (6380): 1094–96.

Lenz, G. (2012). *Follow the Leader? How Voters Respond to Politicians' Policies and Performance.* Chicago: University of Chicago Press.

Lodge, M. and C. S. Taber. (2013). *The Rationalizing Voter.* New York: Cambridge University Press.

Lodge, M. and C. S. Taber. (2006). "Motivated Skepticism in the Evaluation of Political Beliefs." *American Journal of Political Science.* 50 (3): 755–69.

Loftus, E. (1979). "Reactions to Blatantly Contradictory Information." *Memory and Cognition.* 7 (5): 368–74.

Lupia, A. (1994). "Shortcuts Versus Encyclopedias: Information and Voting Behavior in California Insurance Reform Elections." *American Political Science Review.* 88 (1): 63–76.

(1975). "Leading Questions and the Eyewitness Report." *Cognitive Psychology.* 7 (4): 560–72.

and J. C. Palmer. (1974). "Reconstruction of Automobile Destruction." *Journal of Verbal Learning Verbal Behavior*. 13 (5): 585–89.

Lybrand, H. et al. (2019). "How 19 Claims Trump Made During the State of the Union Check Out." Accessed via www.cnn.com/2019/02/05/politics/fact-check-trump-state-of-the-union/ index.html

Mansky, J. (2018.) "The Age-Old Problem of Fake News." *Smithsonian*. Accessed via www.smithsonianmag.com/history/age-old-problem-fake-news-180968945/

Marcus, G. E., W. R. Neuman and M. MacKuen. 2000. *Affective Intelligence and Political Judgment*. Chicago: University of Chicago Press.

Mason, L. 2018. *Uncivil Agreement: How Politics Became Our Identity*. Chicago: University of Chicago Press.

Merola, V. and M. Hitt. (2016.) "Numeracy and the Persuasive Effect of Policy Information and Party Cues." *Public Opinion Quarterly*. 80 (2): 554–62.

Mozur, Paul. (2018.) "A Genocide Incited on Facebook, With Posts From Myanmar's Military." *New York Times*. Accessed via www.nytimes .com/2018/10/15/technology/myanmar-facebook-genocide.html? action=click&module=Top\ percent20Stories&pgtype= Homepage

Mullinx, K. J., T. J. Leeper, J. N. Druckman, and J. Freese. (2015). "The Generalizeability of Survey Experiments." *Journal of Experimental Political Science*. 2: 109–38.

Mutz, D. (2012). "The Great Divide: Campaign Media in the American Mind." *Daedalus*. 141 (4): 83–97.

National Public Radio. (2016). "Fact Check: Trump and Clinton Debate for the First Time." Accessed via www.npr.org/2016/09/26/495115346/fact-check-first-presidential-debate.

New York Times. (2016). "Our Fact Checks of the First Debate." Accessed via www. nytimes.com/2016/09/27/us/politics/fact-check-debate.html

Nyhan, B., E. Porter, J. Reifler, and T. J. Wood. (2017). "Taking Corrections Literally But Not Seriously? The Effects of Information on Factual Beliefs and Candidate Favorability." Working paper. Accessed via https://papers .ssrn.com/sol3/papers.cfm?abstract_id=2995128

and J. Reifler. (2010). "When Corrections Fail." *Political Behavior*. 32 (2): 303–30.

and J. Reifler. (2015). "The Effect of Fact-Checking on Elites: A Field Experiment on U.S. State Legislators." *American Journal of Political Science*. 59 (3): 628–640.

J. Reifler, and P. Ubel. (2013). "The Hazards of Correcting Myths About Health Care Reform." 51 (2): 127–32.

Oreskes, N. and E. K. Conway. (2010). *Merchants of Doubt: How a Handful of Scientists Obscured the Truth on Issues from Tobacco Smoke to Global Warming.* New York: Bloomsbury Press.

Petty, R. and J. Cacioppo. (1986). "The Elaboration Likelihood Model of Persuasion." *Advances in Experimental Social Psychology.* 19: 123–205.

Ponder, D. E. (2017). *Presidential Leverage: Presidents, Approval and the American State.* Stanford: Stanford University Press.

Porter, E., T. J. Wood, and B. Bahador. (Forthcoming). "Can Presidential Misinformation on Climate Change Be Corrected? Evidence from Internet and Phone Experiments." *Research and Politics.*

Porter, E., T. J. Wood, and D. Kirby. (2018). "Sex Trafficking, Russian Infiltration, Birth Certificates, and Pedophilia: A Survey Experiment Correcting Fake News." *Journal of Experimental Political Science.* 5 (2): 159–64.

Prior, M., G. Sood, and K. Khanna. (2015). "You Cannot be Serious: The Impact of Accuracy Incentives on Partisan Bias in Reports of Economic Perceptions." *Quarterly Journal of Political Science.* 10 (4): 489–518.

Rahn, W. (1993). "The Role of Partisan Stereotypes in Information Processing about Political Candidates." *American Journal of Political Science.* 37 (2): 472–96.

Redlawsk, D. P. (2002). "Hot Cognition or Cool Consideration? Testing the Effects of Motivated Reasoning on Political Decision Making." *Journal of Politics.* 64 (4): 1021–44.

Schaffner, B. and C. Roche. (2017). "Misinformation and Motivated Reasoning: Responses to Economic News in a Politicized Environment." *Public Opinion Quarterly.* 81 (1): 86–110.

Silverman, C. (November 26, 2016). "This Analysis Shows How Fake Election News Outperformed Real Election News on Facebook." BuzzFeed. Accesed via www.buzzfeednews.com/article/craigsilverman/viral-fake-election-news-outperformed-real-news-on-facebook

Smidt, C. D. (2017). "Polarization and the Decline of the American Floating Voter." *American Journal of Political Science.* 61 (2): 365–81.

Snyder, T. (2017). *On Tyranny: Twenty Lessons from the Twentieth Century.* New York: Penguin University Press.

Spivak, C. (2011). "The Fact-Checking Explosion." *American Journalism Review.* 32: 38–43.

Stanley, J. (2018). *How Fascism Works: The Politics of Us and Them.* New York: Random House.

Sterling, R. W. and W. C. Scott. (1985). *The Republic of Plato.* New York: W.W Norton and Company.

Taber, C. and M. Lodge. (2006). "Motivated Skepticism in the Evaluation of Political Beliefs." *American Journal of Political Science.* 50 (3): 755–69.

and M. Lodge. (2013). *The Rationalizing Voter.* New York: Cambridge University Press.

Tandoc, E. C., Z. W. Lim, and R. Ling. (2017). "Defining "Fake News." *Digital Journalism.* 6 (2): 137–53.

Teisch, S. (January 6, 1992). "A Government of Lies." *The Nation.* 254 (1): 12–14.

Tillmans, W. (February 28, 2018). "My Two-Year Investigation into the Post-Truth Era." *The Guardian.* Accessed via www.theguardian.com/artandde sign/2018/feb/28/wolfgang-tillmans-what-is-different-backfire-effect

Tversy, A. and D. Kahneman. (1973). "Availability: A Heuristic for Judging Frequency and Probability." *Cognitive Psychology.* 5: 207–32.

Uscinski, J. and R. Butler. (2013). "The Epistemology of Fact Checking." *Critical Review.* 25 (2): 162–80.

Vosoughi, S., D. Roy, and S. Aral. (2018). "The Spread of True and False News Online." *Science.* 359 (6380): 1146–51.

Wintersieck, A. L. (2017). "Debating the Truth: The Impact of Fact-Checking During Electoral Debates." *American Politics Research.* 45 (2): 304–31.

Wood, T. J. and E. Porter. (2018). "The Elusive Backfire Effect: Mass Attitudes' Steadfast Factual Adherence." *Political Behavior.* 1–32.

Woodward, C., H. Yen, and C. Rugaber. (February 9, 2019). "AP Fact Check: Trump swipes progress from Obama era." Associated Press. Accessed via www.apnews.com/3e265c4138d04e22886e6e1818789734

Zaller, J. (1992). *The Nature and Origins of Mass Public Opinion.* New York: Cambridge University Press.

Zaller, J. (2004). "Floating Voters in U.S. Presidential Elections, 1948–2000." In *Studies in Public Opinion: Attitudes, Nonattitudes, Measurement Error and Change.* Edited by W. E. Saris and P. M. Sniderman. Princeton: Princeton University Press.

Zimmerman, J. (February 8, 2017). "It's Time to Give Up on Facts." *Slate.* Accessed via https://slate.com/technology/2017/02/counter-lies-with-emotions-not-facts.html

Acknowledgments

We thank Paul Beck, Joshua Becker, Donald Green, Richard Gunther, Kim Gross, Steven Klein, Marcus Kurtz, William Minozzi, Michael Neblo, Daniel Nichanian, Eric Oliver, John Sides, Megan Wood, Ronit Zemel, and the anonymous reviewers for their comments. We are deeply indebted to Frances Lee, whose stewardship made for a vastly improved project. We thank our collaborators Babak Bahador and David Kirby, and especially Brendan Nyhan and Jason Reifler. We also thank the editors of *Political Behavior* and the *Journal of Experimental Political Science*, which published early versions of several of the studies. Mark McKibbin provided excellent research assistance. George Washington University, the Ohio State University, and the Cato Institute provided funding. Errors and omissions are our own.

Cambridge Elements $\equiv$

American Politics

Frances E. Lee
Princeton University

Frances E. Lee is Professor of Politics at the Woodrow Wilson School of Princeton University. She is author of *Insecure Majorities: Congress and the Perpetual Campaign (2016), Beyond Ideology: Politics, Principles and Partisanship in the U.S. Senate (2009), and coauthor of Sizing Up the Senate: The Unequal Consequences of Equal Representation* (1999).

Advisory Board

About the Series

The Cambridge Elements Series in *American Politics* publishes authoritative contributions on American politics. Emphasizing works that address big, topical questions within theAmerican political landscape, the series is open to all branches of the subfield and activelywelcomes works that bridge subject domains. It publishes both original new researchon topics likely to be of interest to a broad audience and state-of-the-art synthesisand reconsideration pieces that address salient questions and incorporate new dataand cases to inform arguments.

Cambridge Elements ≡

American Politics

Elements in the Series

A full series listing is available at: www.cambridge.org/core/series/elements-in-american-politics

CPSIA information can be obtained
at www.ICGtesting.com
Printed in the USA
LVHW111946220120
644448LV00003B/354

9 781108 705929